AGA

"BIBLICAL COUNSELING"

FOR THE

BIBLE

AGAINST
"BIBLICAL COUNSELING"

FOR THE

BIBLE

Martin and Deidre Bobgan

EastGate Publishers
Santa Barbara, CA 93110

First Printing 1994
Second Printing 1998

AGAINST BIBLICAL COUNSELING: FOR THE BIBLE

Copyright © 1994 Martin and Deidre Bobgan
Published by EastGate Publishers
4137 Primavera Road
Santa Barbara, CA 93110

Library of Congress Catalog Card Number 94-92307
ISBN 0-941717-09-7

Printed in the United States of America

And he gave some, apostles;
and some, prophets;
and some, evangelists;
and some, pastors and teachers;
for the perfecting of the saints,
for the work of the ministry,
for the edifying
of the body of Christ. . . .
(Ephesians 4:11-12)

Contents

1

Is Biblical Counseling Biblical?

"**Against biblical counseling?** I thought you were **for** biblical counseling!" We can hear the chorus of cries from even our closest allies. And, our adversaries will relish the opportunity to use this book as proof positive that we are extremists. We expect this book to be misquoted and misrepresented before it is even read. We ask you to hear us out. Our concerns cannot be stated briefly.

For years we have recommended against psychotherapies and their underlying psychologies. We have severely criticized those Christians who have psychologized the faith. There is a serious competition between whether believers will use

3

psychological or biblical information or a combination of the two. Psychotherapy is merely professionalized conversation that contains the opinions of men and the very wisdom of men against which the Bible warns. While we make no recommendation about medical conditions, we do say that there is no reason to resort to the opinions of men (psychotherapy) when God has given us His Word, His Son, and His Holy Spirit.

In this book we will be critiquing those who propose biblical counseling as an alternative to psychological counseling. In doing this we realize that many of our closest friends in the faith may become upset. They may believe that psychology has so overtaken the church that to turn our criticism to biblical counseling is to abandon the seemingly insurmountable task of continuing to confront the psychologizers in the church.

Be assured, we will continue to criticize the psychologizers. However, we believe this book is a necessary critique of the growing biblical counseling movement in America, which is spreading to other parts of the world alongside psychological counseling. We begin by asking a very simple question: "Is biblical counseling biblical?" Though the question is simple, the answer needs explanation. This book is an attempt to answer that question. It is an analysis of biblical counseling—what it is, rather than what it pretends or even hopes to be.

Confidence Lost

Too many believers (both pastors and lay people) have lost confidence in their ability to minister—especially in the area of personal care. Why are so many Christians afraid to minister to believers who are experiencing problems? Why do pastors feel inadequate to the task of personal pastoring? Why do they send their people to psychologically trained therapists?

Numerous Christians have been indoctrinated and intimidated by the world of psychotherapy. Psychological experts have convinced them that while pastors and fellow believers may be able to minister spiritually, they are not prepared to minister psychologically.

A number of years ago I (Martin) spoke to a group of students at a large seminary. After hearing my concerns about psychological counseling and my appeal to them to minister according to the Word of God rather than according to the wisdom of men, a number of men said: "I am completing my seminary program soon, but I wouldn't know how to counsel a person with problems."

What had their extensive schooling included, about the Bible and practical theology? Had they not learned how to exegete Scripture? To preach and teach the Word? Had they not been schooled in the Gospel of Jesus Christ for salvation and sanctification? Did they not know that the Lord lives in every believer to make the Word effective in that life? Surely they had learned these basics of pastoring. Yet, those men were truly uncertain. Indeed, they had bought the lie that one must know psychological models and counseling methods in order to minister to people experiencing problems. They had evidently become intimidated by pastoral counseling classes that help pastors learn how to minister to minor problems, how to identify "real" problems, and then how to refer people to professional psychological therapists.

After wrestling with this question of ministering to people with problems, one pastor came to the conclusion that pastors do not have to be intimidated by psychological counseling theories and therapies. He contended that pastors were already competent to counsel. If they knew the Bible they had more to offer people than psychologists did. That person is Dr. Jay Adams, who is regarded as the father of the biblical counseling movement.

For years Adams has begun his talks on counseling with a story to illustrate that pastors already have what they need to counsel. They have studied the Word of God and they can trust the Lord to give the wisdom and understanding that come with knowing that Word. Adams has sought to make pastors aware of the fact that they are already empowered by the Lord. And, he urges them to practice biblical theology instead of psychology.

Intimidation?

Since that time, a growing number of Christians have become convinced that there is a biblical way to minister to problems of living. They have become persuaded that the alternative to psychological counseling is biblical counseling. Leaders in the biblical counseling movement have sought to relieve that intimidation from psychology through providing training in biblical counseling. But, now we have a new intimidation brought on by the biblical counseling movement itself.

Intimidation? How can pastors be intimidated by the idea of biblical counseling? Believers, including pastors, are intimidated by biblical counseling models and methods as well as by psychological models and methods. They can feel just as inadequate if they have not had some specialized training in biblical counseling. In fact, the biblical counseling movement has actually disempowered pastors by making them think they need specialized "training." Thus, what was intended to be a help has become a hindrance.

First, Christians thought they couldn't counsel because they were not trained in psychology. Now many think they can't counsel because they are not trained specifically in biblical counseling. Others have said they feel much more secure counseling fellow believers after having taken a class and having a manual to use. Thus increasing numbers of pastors and lay people are seeking training in biblical counseling, when what they really need is knowledge of the Word, understanding the Word, personal obedience to the Word, and confidence to discard all psychotherapy and to use the whole armor of God.

Recently a pastor called and asked about pursuing a degree in biblical counseling. We asked him why he thought he needed this additional training. He said he did not feel equipped to counsel, that he had not been trained in the methods of counseling. He hoped that such training would give him the ability to minister to his flock.

We asked him if he had any concordances, Bible dictionaries, commentaries, and other Bible helps. He answered, "Yes." We asked him if he believed that pastors who had fewer books on their shelves 100 to 300 years ago were equipped to minister to their flocks, or if God had left them without adequate resources.

We asked this pastor if he knew the Word of God, if he knew how to preach the Gospel and teach the Word concerning the on-going walk of the believer in sanctification. He answered, "Yes." We asked him if those pastors 100 to 300 years ago who were educated in the Word of God, preached the Gospel, and taught the Word concerning the on-going walk of the believer in sanctification had adequate resources to minister. He got the point and said, "Of course."

To every pastor or lay person who says, "I need to be trained to counsel biblically," we ask those same questions. Can you preach, teach, or confront an individual with the Gospel message of salvation and sanctification? Can you be used by the Holy Spirit to convert a sinner or reprove one who is saved? Can you come alongside to encourage right-eousness or repentance? Can you give the comfort of the Lord whereby you yourself have been comforted? Can you lead another Christian to the same well of living water from which you drink? Are you willing to think and speak biblically and converse about practical theological matters when needful situations arise?

If your answer is "yes," you don't need biblical counseling programs. If your answer is "no," you still don't need biblical counseling programs. Instead, you need opportunities to learn the Word of God, ponder it, and apply it to your own life. That is practical theology: studying the Bible, thinking about it, and doing it. As believers practice theology in their daily lives they become prepared to minister to one another in the body of Christ. No counseling program can ever prepare a person to minister the counsel of the Lord. Only the Lord can prepare a person—through His Word and then through opportunities (life's circumstances) to practice that Word through loving obedience to Him.

This recent craze to learn certain Bible verses related to certain issues of life is paralytically intimidating to those who desire to minister the Gospel. When pastors and lay people who are spiritually mature and biblically knowledgeable are intimidated into being specially trained in biblical counseling, it is time to call a halt to this recent fad.

The Lord has been faithful to equip His servants to minister the Gospel for salvation and sanctification of believers throughout the centuries. He did all of that without the help of Sigmund Freud, Carl Jung, Alfred Adler and other secular psychological theorists. And, He did all of that without the models and methodologies of the twentieth century biblical counseling movement.

"Wait a minute," you say. "Didn't biblical counseling always exist?"

The Lord's counsel has been around since the creation of Adam. And the Word of God includes much biblical counsel. However, biblical counseling as a system is a twentieth-century phenomenon, which was created as a biblical alternative or replacement to psychological counseling. In the effort to replace the wisdom of men (psychology) with the wisdom of the Word, those of us who attempted to formulate a model and methodology of biblical counseling inadvertently developed biblical counseling programs that more or less emulate or parallel psychological counseling. The attempt to develop biblical counseling confounded and compounded the problem of personal ministry by being a mirror reflection of psychological counseling with special training and techniques. No wonder the integrationists say psychological and biblical counselors do the same thing.

One of the leaders of a well-known biblical counseling training program described the levels of training to us. He said that even Dr. Jay Adams would have to begin at level one, just like anyone else. It is doubtful that Adams is intimidated by such remarks, but this is an example of what causes even the best-trained and committed pastors and lay persons to seek out biblical counseling programs.

We have fostered a similar mentality ourselves by recommending that people obtain such specialized training. But, we hereby reject anything we have previously written that would cause pastors and mature believers to think they are inadequately prepared to minister to fellow believers who are experiencing problems of living.

Any person who can be used by the Holy Spirit to lead another to salvation or along the way of sanctification is competent to be used by God to give wise counsel without needing specialized biblical counseling training.

Not Recommending Biblical Counseling?

We have taken a huge departure in this book. Some of what we say may come as a shock to many. But, we do not take this step lightly. It is with repentance from our own involvement in the biblical counseling movement that we write this book.

You may wonder how we ever came to this point in our concerns about counseling. Perhaps a little background may help. Since the early sixties, in addition to reading and studying the Bible, we have been extensively reading and studying psychology. We noticed that more and more sermons were becoming tinged with elements of psychology and that more and more Christians were becoming trained and licensed to practice psychological counseling.

Beginning in the late sixties people began coming to us with problems of living. What could we do but minister what we knew from the Word of God? Although times of meeting were arranged and problems were confronted, they were times of prayer, Bible study, and fellowship. All of us sought what Scripture said, for we were all seekers at the foot of the cross. No one was considered a "counselor" and no one was considered a "counselee." All of us were simply Christians coming together to meet a challenge. As believers we all drank from the same fountain, both the ones who sought help for specific problems and those who came alongside. While we had to learn to avoid using the psychological notions we knew, we did not attempt to develop any specific theories about personal ministry at that time. We simply came alongside to encourage, remind, pray, exhort, and share God's faithfulness. Thus, while temporarily sharing burdens, each one of us bore our own burden, our own response to God, and our own responsibility before God (Galatians 6:1-5). After all, God indwells each one through the Holy Spirit and thereby enables each one to obey His Word. When we think back to those days, we realize that pastors trusted us to minister in this way because of our past training in psychology. Yet, all the while, we tried to discard that training in favor of ministering the Word of God and trusting Him to do the work.

As we found the faithfulness of God in personal ministry, we thought "biblical counseling" must be the alternative to psychological counseling. We began to teach others what we had learned. We wanted to expose the emptiness of the world's ways so that Christians would gain confidence in the Word of God and the work of the Holy Spirit in ministering to one another. We finally decided to write a book to reveal the darkness of psychological counseling ideologies in the light of Scripture. We expressed many of our concerns in *The Psychological Way/The Spiritual Way* and tried to encourage readers to turn back to the Lord and His Word and to find confidence there rather than in the wisdom of men.[1] By then we had begun a "counseling ministry" in a church. We were training others as "biblical counselors" so that they, too, could minister to "counselees." This began what we now see as a compromise with the world. We thought we had to develop some kind of system of "biblical counseling" as an alternative to the ever-growing popularity of "Christian psychology." After all, there were all those hurting people out there in need of help. We desired to be as biblical as possible, but also as unstructured as possible—to leave God room to work.

By that time we were quite familiar with psychological research as well as with how the Bible could be used in personal ministry. We could identify psychological elements in various individuals' attempts to integrate psychology and Christianity. However, we did not realize that we, too, were copying elements from the world, such as designating the one who comes alongside as a "counselor" and the person in need as the "counselee." We were encouraging "biblical counseling" as a specific ministry in the church with certain individuals designated as "biblical counselors."

No longer were we simply fellow believers seeking God's will. We were falling into the trappings of psychological counseling. We were falling into the trap of appointments, one right after another, just as in psychological counseling. We were elevating this as a special "ministry" in the church with training classes and requirements for becoming "counselors." We were inadvertently developing a type of caste system—with those "trained" to counsel near the top. We were doing all of these things, even though we would say at the end of every seminar on biblical counseling: "The ideal church is one with all the biblical counseling anyone would want, but no one would need it." Our reason for saying that was this: where the Word of God is faithfully preached and the hearers apply that Word to their lives in love and obedience, there is no need for biblical counseling. But, since there is no ideal church, there will continue to be problems of living requiring personal care. At that time we were convinced that the personal care should not be psychology or "Christian psychology," but, rather, "biblical counseling."

Through the years we have continued to write books warning about the dangers and antibiblical aspects of various psychoheresies. In each book we attempted to direct readers back to the sufficiency of Christ, the Word of God, and the work of the Holy Spirit. We were initially accused of being negative. So, to counteract that, we encouraged biblical counseling as a replacement for psychological counseling. However, we are now opposed to the biblical counseling movement for the reasons presented in this book. **We are so concerned that we are no longer recommending any biblical counseling centers or biblical counseling training programs.**

Counselee, Counselor, Conversation

Pastoral care has been part of the church for centuries. Pastoral counseling and biblical counseling as conducted today, however, are not the same as personal ministry in the early church. Most pastoral counseling classes in seminaries embrace and teach various psychological theories and therapies. The term *counseling* carries with it the format of a "counselee," a "counselor," and professionalized conversation centered on a problem within the framework of whatever doctrines are held by the counselor, be they biblical or psychological or both.

Furthermore there are certain inescapable similarities between psychological and biblical counseling. Counseling causes people to focus on themselves and their problems. Counseling often gives the "counselee" center stage in his own drama with a ready listener. Counseling presupposes that the counselor is some kind of expert.

Perhaps it's easier to talk about oneself and one's problems with a caring person who is right there in flesh and blood than to talk to the Lord. Perhaps it's easier to be comforted by a counselor after fifty minutes of talking about oneself than to study Scripture to see what God has to say. Perhaps it's easier to trust the wisdom of a counselor, who must be some kind of "expert," than to trust God to give wisdom. Perhaps it's easier to cast the problem at the feet of a counselor than at the feet of Jesus

While a word spoken at the right time and godly counsel can be extremely helpful, does that justify "counseling" over a period of weeks, months

and even years? While a word of encouragement
may be extremely edifying during a personal trial
and words of consolation may bring comfort to the
grieving heart, the inner work of the Lord is what
brings life and holiness along with encouragement
and comfort. There is a very strong possibility, even
in the best biblical counseling, that the so-called
counselee will focus on self. There is also the possibility that the counselor will stand in the place of
God and will attempt to do the work of the Holy
Spirit.

Problem-Centered Counseling

One of the biggest problems in biblical counseling is that it often focuses on problems rather than
on spiritual sanctification. In attempting to minister to the same issues treated by psychological
counseling, biblical counselors too often focus on
the personal or relational problem rather than on
the individual's relationship to the Lord and the
process of sanctification. Biblical counselors too
often attempt to solve problems at the surface
level, or they attempt to discover something about
the inner man through various methods of exploration. The possible dangers are superficiality,
legalism, and formulas on the one hand, or
attempting to analyze the soul on the other.

Instead of focusing on problems or attempting
to expose the heart, a pastor and his congregation
should be involved in active sanctification, growing
in the fruit of the Spirit, learning to walk according
to the Spirit, with Jesus being the primary focus
and becoming like Him the goal. While this is

surely part of the ministry of individuals who call themselves biblical counselors, too much biblical counseling has become something in addition to sound doctrine and practice. The Bible reveals spiritual issues that underlie behavior. Thus it is entirely unnecessary and unscriptural to use psychological means to gain insight into the inner man or to expose the heart and motivation.

Problem-centered counseling rests on the notion that once problems of living are solved spiritual growth will occur. However, the Bible does not teach that. Instead, the emphasis is on spiritual growth, learning to walk according to the Spirit and growing in the fruit of the Spirit. Rather than problems being the barrier to spiritual growth, spiritual stagnation is the barrier to solving problems. Problem-focused counseling can even serve to postpone spiritual growth. Rather than looking at their problems, believers would do well to look to the Lord and increase their knowledge of Him. "But we all, with open face beholding as in a glass the glory of the Lord, are changed into the same image from glory to glory, even as by the Spirit of the Lord" (2 Corinthians 3:18).

Believers need to learn to come to Christ in the time of need, because only there will they find His will and His way in the situation. Every trial is meant to conform us to the image of Christ. Thus every trial must be brought to Him, not to manipulate or to get one's own way, but to find out what God is doing and wants to do. Yes, there are pastors, teachers, and fellow believers who give wise counsel during times of need. However, one does not have to counsel or be counseled to find wisdom.

Wise counsel should be a natural part of the daily life of the church with believers encouraging, admonishing, exhorting, confronting one another and praying for each other. **All this can be done without a system, center, or ministry of "biblical counseling."** Though the justifiers of biblical counseling would contend otherwise, all of this was done prior to the beginning of the biblical counseling movement only twenty-five years ago, at least in churches that were preaching and teaching the whole counsel of God.

A 20th Century Phenomenon

If biblical counseling is mandated as an essential addition to Christianity, one must raise this question: **What did the church do without the biblical counseling movement for over nineteen centuries?** While institutions have failed, we trust Jesus' promise that He would build His church and that "the gates of hell shall not prevail against it" (Matthew 16:18).

Biblical counseling, with its specialized training and similarities to psychological counseling, is not needed. The Gospel is God's way of salvation and sanctification. God gave ministries to the church, as outlined in His Word, and the very life of Christ indwells the believer. These great and marvelous spiritual realities are God's ways in contrast to man's ways.

Believers do not need biblical counseling texts, workbooks, in-take forms, programs, or specialized training. While some materials may be helpful on occasion and while they may organize aspects of doctrine, they can only be seen as supplementary at best. However, such materials can become a crutch that cripples genuine communication. Moreover, they can limit personal ministry to such a superficial level as to strengthen the flesh and postpone the inner work of the Lord.

If counselors dispense individual Bible verses as pills for particular problems and believers do not feed on the whole Word of God, there will be no growth, only a series of quick fixes at best. The Word of God is both God-breathed and living. It is not a list of isolated verses to be removed from their context and arranged according to problems of living. What Christians need is the whole counsel of God in daily feeding, in thinking through, and in walking according to the Spirit.

If a Christian merely feeds on isolated tidbits applicable to specific problems, he will simply go from problem to problem, isolated verse to isolated verse, and may remain an infant in his faith. In commenting on Proverbs 30:5 and 6 ("Every word of God is pure: he is a shield unto them that put their trust in him. Add thou not unto his words, lest he reprove thee, and thou be found a liar."), Charles Bridges says:

> So wisely has God linked together the several parts of his system, that we can receive no portion soundly, except in connection with the whole. The accuracy of any view is more than suspicious, that serves to put a forced

construction upon Scripture, to dislocate its connection, or to throw important truths into the shade.[2]

Unfortunately, many, who call themselves Christians, want something like what the world offers. They want an alternative that is like psychological counseling, but which would still be within the confines of Scripture. Just as the Israelites desired a king because the nations around them had kings, so Christians desire counseling. They think they need something like the remedy offered by the world. Thus we are extending the range of our concern about the psychologizing of the church to include much of what goes on in biblical counseling.

One of our books, *How to Counsel from Scripture*, encourages biblical counseling. While it is always difficult to repent of anything publicly, it is doubly difficult to repent about something already successfully in print. However, we are repenting of any statements in our past writings that are in conflict with this current book. After reading this book, you will see what it is we oppose and, thus, from what we are repenting.

For years we counseled, trained counselors, and wrote articles and books about both psychological and biblical counseling. We are experienced at biblical counseling, having counseled the gamut of problems from "alcoholism to anorexia" and from "anxiety to xenophobia." Our current response to our past writings and practices will become apparent as you read through the chapters of this book.

Two Major Criticisms

There are two major criticisms in this book. One is directed at biblical counseling practices; the other is directed at the rationale behind biblical counseling. Throughout the world there are those who call themselves "biblical counselors" and refer to what they do as "biblical counseling." There are also numerous organizations that claim to offer biblical counseling. And, there are some that train biblical counselors. **We will be naming a few individuals and organizations as examples, but the problems extend to the other persons and groups involved in biblical counseling.** The more any practice called biblical counseling resembles psychological counseling, the more we oppose it. However, be assured that, although we are taking a stand against biblical counseling as a distinct entity, we continue to encourage and support biblical counsel as part of, rather than apart from, the biblically ordained ministries of the church.

We are against biblical counseling, but we are for biblical counsel given through the ministries of the church as outlined in Ephesians 4:11-16, Romans 12 and elsewhere in Scripture. Biblical counsel is one part of the biblically ordained ministries of the church. Biblical counseling, apart from the biblically ordained ministries of the church, is too narrow a calling with too high a visibility. Neither the calling nor the visibility is biblically justifiable.

While this may sound like no more than a problem of semantics, the errors of biblical counseling are very serious, and they are so intricately woven into the very fabric of biblical counseling that the cloth itself must be discarded. As we unravel this cloth and reveal the worldly threads that must be discarded, we will find that the true threads from God's Word fit best in their original place to be useful for the ministry to the saints and edification of believers.

We know that many people will not be able to accept all we say. Our message is a multiple one. We continue to be totally opposed to psychological counseling, but we are now speaking out against biblical counseling. However, we are, at the same time, confirming the biblically ordained ministries of the church. Even if one cannot accept the entire message of this book, we hope and pray that the errors of biblical counseling will be acknowledged and repented of, especially by those who call themselves "biblical counselors."

2

Biblical Counseling and the Cure of Souls

Throughout the history of the church there has been what was called the "cure of souls." This was the ministry to individuals struggling with problems of living, which included such personal matters as grief over the loss of a loved one, assurance of salvation, confession of sin, and repentance. All dealt with how to live the Christian life and how to overcome sin. However, the emphases varied. Some emphasized the outer, external transgressions of the law of God. Others sought to delve into the inner life of the soul. Pastoral care that dealt mainly with confession and repentance of external transgressions had the possible shortcomings of being external and legalistic, never reaching into the inner person. Pastoral care that focused on the inner life of the soul had the possibility of much speculation as to the content of the soul regarding motivation and lack of faith. It also had the possibility of breeding introspection and preoccupation over one's own spiritual condition. Both extremes, though finding their seeds in Scripture, could lead away from New Testament teachings regarding walking after the spirit rather than after the flesh. Pastoral care focusing on external transgressions could actually help the flesh conform to greater appearances of Christianity without conforming the inner person to the image of Christ. On the other hand, pastoral care focusing on the inner life could lead people away from focusing on Christ to focusing on themselves.

God's Provisions for Believers

Jesus Christ provided all that was necessary for believers to live fruitful lives pleasing to God. He declared: "I am the way, the truth, and the life: no man cometh unto the Father, but by me" (John 14:6). He taught His disciples the truth that would set them free. He died for their transgressions and rose again to give new life, that all who believe in Him might live through His life in them. He sent the Holy Spirit, who makes Christ's work and God's Word effectual in believers. As Peter wrote so clearly:

> Grace and peace be multiplied unto you through the knowledge of God, and of Jesus

our Lord, according as his divine power hath given unto us all things that pertain unto life and godliness, through the knowledge of him that hath called us to glory and virtue: Whereby are given unto us exceeding great and precious promises: that by these ye might be partakers of the divine nature, having escaped the corruption that is in the world through lust (2 Peter 1:2-4).

Besides giving each believer inner resources to live a life pleasing to God, Christ gave to the church "apostles; and some, prophets; and some, evangelists; and some, pastors and teachers" (Ephesians 4:11). He ordained such persons to help believers become more and more like Christ, to progress in their sanctification: "For the perfecting of the saints, for the work of the ministry, for the edifying of the body of Christ: Till we all come in the unity of the faith, and of the knowledge of the Son of God, unto a perfect man, unto the measure of the stature of the fulness of Christ" (Ephesians 4:12,13). Thus we have the beginning of pastoral care and the mutual edification of all believers.

Throughout the Epistles we see evidences of pastoral care as well as doctrinal instruction. The very heart of Paul for pastoral care can be seen in his reference to the Galatian believers as "my little children, of whom I travail in birth again until Christ be formed in you" (Galatians 4:19). To the Thessalonians he wrote: "For ye remember, brethren, our labour and travail: for labouring night and day, because we would not be chargeable unto any of you, we preached unto you the gospel of God" (1 Thessalonians 2:9). But, Paul's passion for Christ in the care of souls was not divorced from truth and righteousness. He had hard things to say when it was necessary to correct error and expose sin.

Besides pastoral care, the mutual care and concern for one another's spiritual and temporal well-being in the early church involved all believers. They were to love, encourage, edify, exhort, admonish, forgive, and restore one another. Thus, from the very beginning, the priesthood of all believers was an active office, which included sharing goods and meals, bearing one another's burdens, praying for one another, and "forbearing one another in love; endeavoring to keep the unity of the spirit in the bond of peace" (Ephesians 4:2,3).

While ongoing pastoral care and mutual care for one another had much to do with teaching, encouraging and edifying, it also had to do with handling problems and dealing with sin in the lives of believers. Lest we form a romantic view of the early church, the Bible records problems of living in a community of like-minded believers. There were Christians sinning against other Christians, which provided opportunities to learn to forgive as Christ forgives. While all believers had the life of Christ in them, they did not always act according to that life. Reproof, conviction of sin, confession, repentance, and forgiveness were necessary from the very beginning of Christianity and continue to this day. Therefore, the care of souls ended up being referred to as the "cure of souls."

The "Cure of Souls"

In his book *A History of the Cure of Souls*, John T. McNeill says: "The cure of souls is, then, the sustaining and curative treatment of persons in those matters that reach beyond the requirements of animal life."[1] This "cure of souls" began early in the church with various writings on such aspects of the Christian life as grief, consolation, repentance, discipline, guidance, and growth. The medieval system emphasized legal restraint of external "sins" rather than sin residing in the inner man. The Protestant Reformation emphasized the inner man without ignoring the external expressions.

One of the primary elements of the cure of souls was the exercise of church discipline for grave offenses. However, documents from the second and third centuries indicate that there was no single system for dealing with those Christians who committed such serious sins as idolatry, unchastity, and bloodshed. Some churches attempted to restore the sinner; others allowed only one repentance for serious sin; and still others simply excommunicated the sinner by applying the Scripture about the sin unto death from 1 John 5:16. Some churches required public confession of sin and public repentance. Others allowed for private confession, but exercised public humiliation.[2] Yet, the overall care of souls was not neglected. A sermon of Augustine included the following words:

> Disturbers are to be rebuked, the low-spirited to be encouraged, the infirm to be supported, objectors confuted, the treacher-

ous guarded against, the unskilled taught, the lazy aroused, the contentious restrained, the haughty repressed, litigants pacified, the poor relieved, the oppressed liberated, the good approved, the evil borne with, and all are to be loved. (*Sermo* ccix)[3]

From the sixth to the sixteenth century the means of confession and penance were highly influenced by a body of literature referred to as the Penitential Books. These manuals, primarily written by Welsh and Irish monks, were used extensively by parish priests in ministering to people in various moral or spiritual predicaments.[4] They included much detail concerning various sins and acts of piety, which could be practiced as a form of penance. By listing sins and their opposite virtues, the writers hoped to bring about spiritual restitution. For instance, the sin of greed could be "cured" by the act of giving.[5] In what were referred to as the "better books," much emphasis was given on how a confessor was to treat a confessant as a fellow sinner. Also, some of the books instructed the confessor to lead the confessant step by step through doctrine to examine the faith of the confessant.[6]

Unfortunately, however, outside influences entered and the seeds of the indulgences were sown with provisions for a sinner to pay a surrogate to do penance for him.[7] Another problem with the Penitential Books was the number of discrepancies among them. What called for severe punishment in one might require a slight penance in another. The books were copied and altered so that there was little consistency among them. While they were very authoritative on their own as far as administration and compliance in a particular parish, they lacked official ecclesiastical authorization.

By the twelfth century private confession with specific forms of penance was developing into a sacramental system with priests being the primary administrators of absolution. In the early thirteenth century the Fourth Lateran Council required every adult to confess to his priest annually.[8] Pope Gregory IX (1227-1241) also allowed Franciscan and Dominican Friars to hear confession and offer absolution.[9] These friars actively participated in the care of souls, gave advice, heard confessions, and offered remedies. Although this activity started out as care and concern for souls, it later deteriorated through untrustworthy friars and the widespread sale of indulgences.

The Reformation and the Care of Souls

Also, during the latter part of the Middle Ages, more people were learning to read, and clerics were writing books explaining doctrine and encouraging morality. This presented possibilities for lay people both to learn and to minister to one another. Some of the writings taught that all Christians were responsible to care for one another both physically and spiritually. This meant they were to correct their neighbors, encourage righteousness, and edify one another in the faith.[10] With the invention of the printing press and more broadly spread literacy, many were ready for the Reformation.

Even during the Reformation, Luther continued to believe in the importance of confession. However, he made dramatic changes. He did not agree that confession should consist of a detailed recitation of a litany of sinful acts. Instead, he taught that confession should focus more on sin as a condition of the soul, and he emphasized the grace of God to absolve the repentant sinner. Rather than limiting the role of confessor to the clergy, Luther taught that confession could be made to another believer. With renewed emphasis on the authority of Scripture and the priesthood of all believers, Christians found their resources for ministering to one another.

Books were also being written by other reformers on doctrine and ministry. The cry of "Sola Scriptura" affected the care of souls as well as theology and preaching. The care of souls had to do with applying Scripture in the lives of believers as well as the continued practice of confession, repentance, and restoration. The more a person knew and applied Scripture in his own life through the ministry and fruit of the Holy Spirit, the more that person was equipped to give counsel to fellow believers. Because of the reemphasis on the priesthood of all believers, there was a renewed emphasis on mutual encouragement, admonition, confession, and forgiveness. Earnest pastors regularly visited members of their churches to encourage devotion, offer counsel, hear confession, and propose penitential remedies. Of course all of this was within the context of evangelizing the lost and preaching and teaching the word to assembled believers and possible converts. The pastor had great opportunity to teach and preach to many at once, but even the most conscientious ones were limited by time available for personal counsel. John Calvin described the pastoral role this way:

> The office of a true and faithful minister is not only publicly to teach the people over whom he is ordained pastor, but as far as may be, to admonish, exhort, rebuke and console each one in particular.[11]

Besides the doctrine of the priesthood of all believers, qualifying members of the body of Christ to minister to one another, the reformers emphasized the responsibility of the believer to search himself concerning inner sinfulness. Furthermore, the reformers taught that confession should be made to God, though the confession could be in the presence of a fellow believer. Huldreich Zwingli wrote: "Auricular confession is nothing but a consultation, in which we receive from him whom God has appointed . . . advice as to how we can secure peace of mind."[12]

The English reformers also stressed repentance, and when they used the word *penance* they were not referring to the sacramental system of penance, but rather to repentance. They also taught that one could not be forgiven until he repented of the wrong. The early Presbyterians elected elders to help with procedures regarding admonition, correction, and restoration. The Puritans emphasized godly living through preaching, writing and personal counsel. Extensive republishing of Puritan works during our present century reveals the importance given to the state of the individual soul and practical devotion. Richard Baxter's *A Christian Directory* gave detailed instructions regarding Christian morality, conscience, behavior, devotion, correction, and restoration.[13] Preachers sought to awaken the Christian conscience and instructed believers in practical godly living. The purpose of personal counsel was primarily to help those who were struggling with sin and to bring them to repentance and restoration.

The Puritans and the Idolatrous Heart

Since the Reformers contended that disobedience to God's law was idolatry of the heart, they attempted to cure disobedient sinners through curing their hearts. Church historian E. Brooks Holifield says:

> The Puritan pastor, especially in the seventeenth century, became a specialist in the cure of the idolatrous heart. He analyzed motives, evaluated feelings, sought to discern hidden intentions and to direct inward consent.[14]

Methods consisted of not only analyzing the condition of the soul, but also choosing appropriate words to teach truth. First they had to discover the inner state of a person and then bring about the remedy. This was all done through questioning and then setting forth arguments to bring a person to repentance.

Besides differences in method, there were differences in emphasis. Pastors relied on revelation and reason in their analysis and argument, but they did not always agree on the relationship between reason and emotion and between the understanding and the will. In other words, should the pastor appeal to the person's reason or his emotion? Could he rely on the will to follow the understanding? How much was the will dependent on God's grace?[15]

Puritans also believed the cure of souls and spiritual growth consisted of believers going through different stages or levels. Sanctification was an ongoing process of going through stages of growth aided by the help of pastors who could supposedly identify the stage of the inner life's progress.[16] Holifield says:

> Pious New Englanders, especially, wanted to learn how to map their progress, and the Puritan pastors became masters of introspection, cartographers of the inner life, adept at recognizing the signs of salvation.[17]

Nearly all of the Protestant Christians expected pastors to know about the intricacies of the inner life and to be able to interpret and analyze them so they could proceed on their inner spiritual development.[18]

The Great Awakening and Pastoral Care

With the Great Awakening of the eighteenth century in America came theological disagreements regarding how one could judge the inner life of those who professed faith in Christ. Some believed that a "holy life" was enough evidence, but others contended that it was necessary for a pastoral judgment to determine the true state of the soul. Those who sought to know the interior life attempted to discover hidden affections by questioning believers about their inner feelings.[19] However, Holifield says:

> In reaction against such "enthusiasm," the ministers who disliked all the pastoral probing at "passions and affections" charged that churches were being uncharitable when they required evidence of inward conversion, and presumptuous when they attempted to judge it.[20]

Through the years prior to the twentieth century the word *psychology* had to do with the study of the soul, primarily from a theological perspective. The conflicting ideas about the nature of the will, inner motivation, passions, and reason were argued from various biblical perspectives, along with subjective observation and current philosophical works. There was a growing interest in understanding the inner person—why people do what they do and how they change. As pastors and theologians worked to increase both inner and outer godliness, many became more preoccupied with the study of the soul than with the study of God. Even books on theology changed their order of things so that the theology of man took on greater and greater importance. Theologians previous to Friedrich Schleiermacher of Germany generally considered theology to be the study of God, and that from knowing God one could gain insight into His creation, including the nature of man.[21] However, Schleiermacher included self-consciousness in his theology, whereby subjective experience gained a foothold alongside revelation. He understood piety to be the "feeling of absolute dependence," by which he meant a consciousness of self's dependence on God.[22]

Influences of the World

The nineteenth century saw the development of pastoral theology as it embraced various forms of mental philosophy. Mental philosophy and natural theology joined hands. Christian apologetics depended upon the reasoning of the natural mind to discover the existence of God. By using natural science and mental philosophy to "prove" God and by using reason and sentiment to influence the will, pastoral theology was becoming prepared to embrace twentieth-century clinical psychology. There was already a great deal of interest in studying the mind in relation to the will and how to influence the will both directly and indirectly.[23] With the rising interest in studying the mind and soul, there was a gradual shift from learning about creation (including mankind) through knowing the

Creator to studying creation by other means. The rise of science encouraged this trend, so that America was ready to swallow all kinds of speculation about the nature of the human, what lies beyond appearances, and why people do what they do.

Mesmerism, with its seeming ability to access untapped powers of the mind, influenced the way Americans, including Christians, would view themselves. Charles Poyen, who brought mesmerism to America during the 1830s, impressed his audiences with hypnotized subjects who spontaneously engaged in what appeared to be mental telepathy, precognition, and clairvoyance.[24] Anton Mesmer's original theories had to do with what he called "animal magnetism," which was supposedly an invisible bodily fluid influencing both physical and mental health. His early method involved an attempt to influence that fluid by moving magnets across the body of a person immersed in water. His followers, however, discovered they could obtain the same results with mere suggestion, without the magnets or water. Through the use of hypnotic suggestion, people entered trance-like states. Some experienced deeper states of trance in which they claimed to feel utter unity with the universe. Some gave apparent supernatural information and appeared to diagnose diseases telepathically. Thus, mesmerism presented possibilities of a great potential of untapped powers and healing within the mind.

Followers of Mesmer promoted notions of hypnotic suggestion, healing through talking, and mind-over-matter and thereby influenced the development of psychotherapy (healing through conversation), hypnosis, and positive thinking—all fountains at which twentieth-century pastoral counselors would drink. Mesmerism greatly affected the early development of psychiatry through Jean-Martin Charcot, Pierre Janet, and Sigmund Freud, all of whom used information gleaned from patients in the hypnotic state, as they developed their theories.[25]

Hypnosis, practiced for centuries in various occult activities, including medium trances, had now gained respectability and entered Western medicine with its suggestions of unseen reservoirs of power within the mind. And, the seeds of positive thinking were planted for Norman Vincent Peale and Robert Schuller to harvest a century later.

Mesmer's far reaching influence gave an early impetus to scientific-sounding religious alternatives to Christianity. Mesmerism suggested powers that could be used to understand the self, attain perfect health, develop supernatural gifts, and reach spiritual heights. It was the early stimulus for the human potential movement and positive thinking religion, as well as other mind-science religions. In his book *Mesmerism and the American Cure of Souls*, Robert Fuller describes how mesmerism held promises for self improvement, spiritual experience, self-discovery, and human potential, without having to rely on the God of the Bible. He contends that mesmerism was "the first psychological system to provide individuals with curative services that have traditionally been classified under the rubric *cure of souls*."[26]

Psychiatrist Dr. Thomas Szasz, who contends that all psychotherapy is fake religion, says:

> Insofar as psychotherapy as a modern "medical technique" can be said to have a discoverer, Mesmer was that person. . . . Mesmer stumbled onto the literalized use of the leading scientific metaphor of his age for explaining and exorcising all manner of human problems and passions, a rhetorical device that the founders of modern depth psychology subsequently transformed into the pseudomedical entity known as psychotherapy.[27]

Thus we have a fake religion posing as a true religion replacing the cure of souls for some and contaminating the cure of souls for others. Pastoral training was soon to include psychotherapy.

Compromising the Faith

During the latter half of the nineteenth century, Christian faith and the authority of the Bible were being challenged by a combination of factors: Darwinian evolution, Freudian theories of a powerful unconscious driving behavior, and seeming contradictions between science and the Bible. In response, a large number of Christians adjusted their faith to accommodate those so-called scientific discoveries. To avoid conflict between the wisdom of the world and the Word of God, they reduced the Bible to not much more than a story book, turned Jesus into an ethical example, and based their faith on good works and religious feelings.[28] James Turner, in his book *Without God, Without Creed*, shows how Christian leaders inadvertently encouraged disbelief in God while trying to rescue the faith. He says:

> In trying to adapt their religious beliefs to socioeconomic change, to new moral challenges, to novel problems of knowledge, to the tightening standards of science, the defenders of God slowly strangled Him. If anyone is to be arraigned for deicide, it is not Charles Darwin but his adversary Bishop Samuel Wilberforce, not the godless Robert Ingersoll but the godly Beecher family.[29]

Protestants of the liberal-modernist persuasion were more ready and eager to embrace the new teachings of psychology than those who still believed in the authority and truth of Scripture for doctrine and faith. Holifield says:

> By the end of the century the mainline liberals concluded that the key to unlocking the mysteries of religion and reality was "in ourselves."[30]

Psychologist William James's teachings were very appealing, especially those about the dominance of the will and the importance of habit.[31] James also wrote about introspection, the "subliminal self," and transformations through religious experience. He did not care what kind of religion or about any kind of doctrine, but that did not seem to bother clergy of the more liberal persuasion. Shortly after the turn of the century there was a direct attempt to bring psychological principles together with Christianity. This was the Emmanuel Movement, which was started by Episcopalians. They were eclectic and drew from a variety of available sources, including Freud, Janet, and James. Their methodology seemed to vacillate between attempting to work indirectly through the subconscious and to appeal directly to the will through reasoned discourse. One can see the influence of mesmerism in their use of relaxation techniques with positive suggestions. They desired to develop a "pastoral psychotherapy" that would strengthen character through tapping into the hidden powers of the subconscious. And, they justified their use of secular psychotherapy by saying that all pastors practiced psychotherapy whether they recognized it or not. [32]

Psychological explorations, explanations, and experiences took hold of the American psyche during the first half of this century as the study of the soul ensconced itself within the disciplines of science and medicine. John Dewey, who is known for his designs to change society through progressive education, worked to connect values to science rather than to God. Philosopher Dr. Gordon Clark says in his analysis of Dewey's teachings:

Running through much of Dewey's writing is
the theme that morality is or should be
made continuous with science. The experi-
mental method should be transferred from
the technical field of physics and applied to
the wider field of human life. Standards of
conduct, he says, are very largely to be had
from the findings of the natural sciences.
Education and morals are to advance along
the same road that the chemical industry
has traveled. And the success of science in
limited fields is the promise of effecting integration in the wider field of collective human
experience.[33]

Dewey's theme of "adjustment" between human
beings and their environment influenced the cure
of souls as well as education.[34]

Psychological Pastors

As psychology increased in popularity, pastors
were feeling less and less successful at inspiring
their flocks to support the work of the ministry.
Therefore some pastors turned to psychology in
their attempt to improve their care of souls and
enhance their sermons. Two very liberal men led
the way: Norman Vincent Peale and Harry Emer-
son Fosdick. Peale actively included psychiatric
teachings and practices both in his preaching and
in creating a "religion-psychiatric clinic" along with
a Freudian psychiatrist.[35] Fosdick blended the
doctrines of psychology with elements of Christian
living in his famous sermons. Holifield declares:

Fosdick was a living illustration of the burgeoning therapeutic sensibility. Under his tutelage a generation of ministers constructed topical sermons on the mastery of depression, the conquest of fear, the overcoming of anxiety, and the joys of self-realization.[36]

The practical attempt at integrating psychology and Christianity was primarily begun by pastors of mainline liberal churches. In their attempt to please their flocks by using the latest theories of psychology, pastors opened the way for professional psychologists to care for their flocks. Pastoral theology classes included ideas of Freud, Alfred Adler, Carl Jung, Erich Fromm, Carl Rogers, Abraham Maslow, Rollo May and others. The doctrines of these men, though at variance with Scripture, were incorporated because of their seeming scientific status. Pastoral counseling textbooks written by pastoral counseling professors included the personality theories of those men. Rogers' "client-centered" therapy was particularly appealing to pastors, but they also used psychoanalytic and behavioristic personality theories along with those of humanistic psychology. Thus many pastors assumed therapeutic roles and provided acceptance and understanding in place of confronting the sinner and guiding him to repentance. By the middle of the century most seminaries offered classes in psychology.[37] These included seminaries of conservative, as well as liberal, denominations.

Many Christians continued to turn to their pastors in time of personal distress. Pastors tried to apply various psychological methodologies as they attempted to help people. However, many of them did not find the success they were expecting. Then, rather than seeking the Lord and His Word for answers to their dilemma, they often chose other paths, which included getting more training in psychology and referring their people out to professional therapists. Mental health associations worked hard to convince pastors that while they might be able to help people with limited problems, they could cause great harm if they did not refer more serious cases to professionals.

One of the primary objectives of the National Association for Mental Health was to provide: "Effective community information and education services to help people know the nature of mental illness, better understand the mentally ill, and know where to go for help." To meet that objective they held "information and educational services for clergy."[38] Local branches arranged meetings for mental health professionals and pastors to get together to help one another. The primary persons helped, however, were the professional therapists who helped themselves to the pastors' flocks. Pastors felt intimidated by their own lack of psychological expertise and, thus, became willing to refer their people to those therapists who attended meetings. To this day, many professional therapists make it a point to contact pastors for possible referrals.

"Psychological Awakening" of Evangelicals

With the field of psychological counseling exploding and pastors referring their flocks to professional therapists came the great "psychological awakening" of evangelical Christianity. If pastors must send their flocks to professional psychotherapists, then there was a crying need for Christians to become trained in psychology and psychiatry. After all, pastors did not want to lose their people to "godless" psychologists and psychiatrists, who might not appreciate Christianity. Thus began the era of so-called "Christian psychology," which simply refers to psychology being practiced by professing Christians. While there is no form of clinical psychology that is "Christian psychology,"[39] what falls under that designation has been embraced by numerous pastors and has captured the minds and hearts of countless Christians.

The best-known evangelical who took advantage of the situation is Clyde Narramore, whose book *The Psychology of Counseling* has been used as a textbook in seminaries and Bible colleges since 1960. In that book he teaches pastors how to use psychological knowledge in their pastoral care and instructs them to refer serious cases to professional psychotherapists. He promotes the idea that a competent pastor is one who knows when to refer his flock to psychologists and psychiatrists. He contends that "the minister who can detect the symptoms of a serious mental illness can perform an important function in helping his people seek early professional care."[40]

Narramore helped transform the sense of failure experienced by many pastors into an acceptable liaison between professionals: professional evangelical pastors and professional mental health specialists. He was also instrumental in encouraging young believers to become mental health professionals. James Dobson credits Clyde Narramore for guiding him towards becoming a licensed psychologist.[41] Others joined the ever-expanding ranks of "Christian psychologists." Seminaries, not content to train pastors in psychological counseling theories and techniques, added graduate schools to train psychotherapists. They hoped that by joining psychology with Christianity they could offer Christians the best of both worlds.

20th Century Biblical Counseling Movement

In the meantime there were some pastors and other Christians who found serious problems with the use of psychological counseling theories and techniques. They noticed serious contradictions between the doctrines of Scripture and the various psychological teachings. After all, the secularists who originally devised the psychological counseling theories and therapies not only eroded confidence in Scripture; they were opposed to the doctrines of Christianity. Besides the obvious contradictions, these concerned pastors and other concerned believers saw that psychology was usurping the place of theology, that the focus of attention was becoming self rather than God, that psychology was limited to working with what the Bible refers to as flesh, and that Christianity itself was becoming psychologized. These Christians were not sold on psychology. They were not convinced that the integration of psychology and the Scriptures was really any more possible than joining light with darkness. What could they offer as an alternative to psychological counseling?

In his book *Competent to Counsel*, Dr. Jay Adams describes his own struggle over the issue of Christians using the psychological theories and therapies of the world. After having been acutely exposed to the psychological process during a summer fellowship under Dr. O. Hobart Mowrer's leadership, Adams concluded that Christians have something superior to psychological counseling theories and therapies. Christians have what they need in the Scriptures. Out of his struggles, Adams developed what he calls Nouthetic Counseling, which consists of confronting a believer with the Word of God for the purpose of change.

Adams expressed his concern about the usual practice of pastoral counseling when he wrote:

> Sadly, it is not only liberal pastors who give non-scriptural counsel these days. Some men, who preach the Bible in their pulpits, change their tune when they enter the counseling room. They may have been taught in seminary to counsel psychologically (i.e., according to worldly wisdom and ways) rather than scripturally. They may mix the two. Be alert; not all Christian counselors do Christian counseling.[42]

Adams worked hard to encourage pastors to use the Bible instead of the psychological opinions of men and to provide biblical counseling information. In 1981 he wrote:

> Over the past 12 years I have worked assiduously to produce a body of literature in a field that, **prior to that time, virtually did not exist: the field of biblical counseling.**[43] (Emphasis added.)

Adams worked to develop a theology of counseling from Scripture, rather than a psychology of counseling from the secular systems.

Besides Adams there were others who were attempting to counsel from Scripture. Biblical counseling seemed to be the only alternative to psychological counseling. At least it was another option. But, where might a person find a biblical counselor among the vast numbers of Christian counselors? Thus came attempts to train biblical counselors. Adams was joined by Dr. John Bettler to establish the Christian Counseling and Educational Foundation (CCEF). Adams was also instrumental in forming the National Association of Nouthetic Counselors (NANC). John Broger developed counseling manuals and formed the Biblical Counseling Foundation (BCF). Numerous other groups and organizations attempted to teach and provide biblical counseling, such as the International Association of Biblical Counselors (IABC).

Biblical counseling is a growing movement in this country, even though it is minuscule in

comparison to the gargantuan army of psychologically trained "Christian counselors." But, what is
called "biblical counseling" is not always biblical.
For instance, practicing psychologists and psychiatrists often refer to what they are doing as "biblical
counseling."

Integrationists, using the models and methods
of counseling psychology along with the Bible, often
refer to themselves as "biblical counselors." For
example, Dr. Larry Crabb, whose psychological
teachings we have critiqued, considers himself a
biblical counselor, and his organization is called the
Institute of Biblical Counseling.[44] Even some of
the counselors who would be considered "biblical
counselors" by a more stringent definition continue
to use psychological "tools," such as various personality tests and inventories. Counselors who take
classes in biblical counseling often simply add what
they learn to whatever psychological models and
methods they are already using. Others, have
absorbed psychological notions through simply living in a psychologized society and attending psychologized schools.

The largest and probably the fastest growing
organization of Christian counselors is the American Association of Christian Counselors (AACC).
There are thousands of professionals who are
members of the AACC, and on their advisory board
are some of the best-known psychologizers of
Christianity. The AACC describes itself as a group
of "professional, pastoral, and lay counselors who
are equally committed to psychological excellence
and biblical truth."[45] These individuals regard

themselves as Christian counselors and many would refer to themselves as "biblical counselors." We think it fair to say that none would regard themselves as being in violation of Scripture. Although we regard what the psychologizers do as psychoheresy, we have never met one who viewed their psychological counseling as anything but biblical.

In an article in *Today's Better Life*, psychiatrist Frank Minirth says:

> If you feel you or a family member needs counseling, don't put it off. Finding and going to a competent, **biblical counselor** may take time and effort, but it's an important investment for your future health and happiness.
>
> Experts estimate that there are more than 200 distinct counseling approaches based on various personalities, theologies, psychological orientations, values, and personal experiences—all labeled "Christian."
>
> . . .
>
> Whatever kind of counseling you choose, make sure you seek the help of a competent, **biblical counselor.** Most Christian therapists model their techniques after Jesus Christ, the master counselor who demonstrated perfect balance.[46] (Emphasis added.)

Minirth has simply substituted the words *biblical counselor* for Christian psychologist.

One can see how corrupted the term *biblical counselor* has become. Minirth lists numerous psychological "credentials, certifications, licensures, and professional organizations" to look for when seeking a "biblical counselor."[47] The article by Minirth is an excellent example of how perverted and deceptive the term *biblical counselor* has become and why we must abandon the term all together.

Influence of Worldy Wisdom

Every century saw departures from the pure doctrines of Scripture and the inclusion of cultural influences in the "cure of souls." For instance, when it came to pastoral care and other duties, some clergy borrowed from Greek philosophers in about the same way current Christians borrow from psychologists. Rather than simply gleaning from Scripture, St. Ambrose was shown to be "heavily indebted to Cicero" in his book *On the Duties of the Clergy.* McNeill contends that St. Ambrose linked "the four classical virtues, prudence or wisdom, justice, fortitude and temperance" with "the Christian virtues of faith, hope and love." He declares: "This important treatise is a capital example of the integration of the loftiest elements in pagan ethics with the spirit of Christianity."[48] However, borrowing from Cicero, was not necessary, because every one of those so-called "classical virtues" is already in Scripture, and they reduce the Christian life to one of humanistic morality.

The same is true today. Pagan discoveries about human nature that happen to resemble Scripture are not necessary. Moreover, they can draw a person away from God and into self effort. There is a great difference between virtues practiced by a pagan and the seemingly same virtues practiced by one who is walking according to the Spirit. The difference is the source, self or God. Another example of a departure from Scripture was the use of the Penitential Books. The authors of the penitentials did not limit themselves to Scripture. They also included aspects of pre-Christian asceticism.[49]

Since most of the current books about counseling and about Christian living are filled with psychological assumptions and pronouncements, many who want to counsel biblically have turned to some of the Puritan books. The Puritans worked hard at holy living and personal ministry. However, even their books must be read with an element of caution. Though they attempted to understand the nature of man and to systematize godly living, they occasionally gave unbiblical advice addressing problems of living. For instance, in *Baxter's Practical Works: A Christian Directory* the following question and answer are presented:

> *Quest.* But what if I have a necessity of marrying, and can get none but an ungodly person?
> *Answ.* If that be really your case, that your necessity be real, and you can get no other, I think it is lawful.[50]

Also, the Puritan's focus on the interior life of the soul has led at least one historian to credit the Puritans for setting the scene for psychological counseling. Indeed, they were concerned about the state of the soul and took an active interest in the progress of the Christian life. However, the accusation is not fully warranted, because psychology attempts to study the soul apart from the authority of the Bible and apart from faith in the God of the Bible. Yet, one aspect of what Holifield says about the connection between the Puritans and psychology is a distinct possibility. He says:

> American pastoral care traditions are rooted in an ancient introspective piety which demands that Christian clergy possess a knowledge of the inner world. It would not be outrageous to suggest that the extraordinary preoccupation with psychology in twentieth-century America owes something to the heritage of experiential piety; that America became a nation of psychologists in part because it had once been a land of Pietists.[51]

That is troubling because if psychological counseling grew out of the soil of Puritan pastoral care, so biblical counseling, as an entity in itself, may provide the soil for subtleties of psychology to come in and contaminate what is intended to be pure. In an eagerness to develop counseling principles and methods to meet the challenges of the counseling setting, those who desire to remain biblical are nevertheless tempted to see in Scripture notions that originated outside Scripture.

Even now, there are biblical counselors who are eager to explore the inner man. They, too, would like to "possess a knowledge of the inner world." They are no longer satisfied to confront individuals on the basis of external behavior, but want to judge motivation. They, like the Puritans, want to become specialists in curing the idolatrous heart by evaluating feelings and analyzing motives. Thus the tension continues between the external and the internal. There is always the danger of only looking on the external and of becoming legalistic. There is also the danger of speculating about a person's heart regarding motivation. There is a further possibility of encouraging ungodly introspection and preoccupation over one's own psyche.

While twentieth-century biblical counselors are also struggling with the same problems as their predecessors—of attempting to identify sin (external and internal) and to bring about repentance and change—**the cure of souls has never before looked like today's biblical counseling scene**. Even though there is a broad spectrum of what might be called "biblical counseling" with some counseling being more biblical in content and approach than other counseling, the question that must be addressed is this. Is biblical counseling, as it is generally practiced in this present century, biblical? Can it be found in the Old or New Testament? The early church? The Reformation? The Puritan church? Or is it a phenomenon of our times, born out of attempts to offer an alternative to psychological counseling?

In the effort to provide something in the place of psychological counseling, certain practices have been adapted from the therapeutic world. And, there is always the temptation to borrow ideas and methods from the ways of the world. Therefore much biblical counseling looks like psychological counseling at least in structure and often in content. The more it resembles psychological counseling, the further away it is from the intent of the Lord. The closer any ministry in the body of Christ clings to biblical theology in both doctrine and practice, the less it will resemble psychological counseling.

Today's Challenge

We agree with much of what Jay Adams has written. He stresses the counsel of God and makes biblically sound applications for problems of living. However, we must also credit him with starting the biblical counseling movement.[52] While we are in agreement with his intent to help pastors, we are in disagreement with the result. **We are opposed to biblical counseling ministries that operate outside the church, those that function as separate entities inside churches, and all organizations that train biblical counselors for ministries that are visibly separated from the biblically ordained ministries of the church.**

Those who are seeking to minister biblically in the body of Christ have a tremendous challenge before them: to remain true to the Word in both doctrine and practice. Biblical counseling will serve as a slippery slope right back into psychological counseling if it is not brought back under the ministries Christ gave to the church:

> . . . apostles; and some, prophets; and some, evangelists; and some, pastors and teachers; for the perfecting of the saints, for the work of the ministry, for the edifying of the body of Christ: Till we all come in the unity of the faith, and of the knowledge of the Son of God, unto a perfect man, unto the measure of the stature of the fulness of Christ (Ephesians 4:11-13).

This is the place for pastoral care and the mutual edification of all believers, under the authority of the foundation laid by the apostles and prophets as given by Jesus Christ: after the work of the evangelists, under the guidance of pastors and teachers in doctrine and practice, and within the mutual ministry of the saints one to another, for the purpose of building up the body of Christ through mutual encouragement, admonition, confession, repentance, forgiveness, restoration, and counsel.

3

Biblical Counseling and the Bible

There is a mystique about being a counselor. For whatever reason and in spite of various criticisms of psychotherapy and psychotherapists, the overall impression is one of admiration. Americans love counselors and counseling so much that:

> Americans participated in an estimated 100 million therapy sessions with licensed practitioners in the year ending June, 1992, and paid approximately $8.1 billion, not counting prescription drugs, to relieve this national despair.[1]

The role of psychotherapist or counselor is both much admired and much sought after. There are now more than 247,000 psychiatrists, clinical psychologists, social workers, marriage and family therapists, and professional counselors. That does not include psychiatric nurses, school counselors, or pastoral counselors.[2] According to Dr. Bernie Zilbergeld:

> There are more professional therapists than librarians, fire fighters, or mail carriers, almost twice as many therapists as dentists or pharmacists.[3]

In his book *The Psychological Society*, Martin Gross says:

> This book is about the most anxious, emotionally insecure and analyzed population in the history of man, the citizens of the contemporary Psychological Society.[4]

The therapist/counselor role is a prestigious one. Many Christians admire professional counselors for ministering to the malaise of mankind. The counselor himself achieves significance merely by being the one who is looked to when help is needed. We all know the predictable response when one encounters problems of living. The predictable litany is the dialogue of "I have a problem—You need a counselor." And, "professional counseling" is generally what is meant.

Some in the church, however, are concerned about the use of secular theories and therapies. But rather than simply urging people to return to God and His Word, they are offering an alternative form of counseling. They are providing what they call "biblical counseling" instead of psychological counseling. Instead of using psychological means of dealing with problems of living, they claim to use biblical means. And just as the psychological counseling movement is growing, so is the biblical counseling movement. There are now numerous individuals who claim to be biblical counselors, and various teachings on biblical counseling are readily available. But, is biblical counseling biblical?

Old Testament "Counsel"

The best source for the answer is, of course, the Bible. And, a good place to start is a concordance. (All biblical references in this section are from the King James translation.) In the Old Testament there are just five English words (translated from a number of Hebrew words) which seem to relate to the currently used term *counseling*. They are *counsel, counselled, counsellor, counsellors*, and *counsels*. The words translated as *counsellor* and *counsellors* are used in reference to the person giving the counsel. The other ones have to do with what is counseled.

There are at least two ways to examine these words: in their original meaning and in their context. The most often used word and its derivatives can be translated as "advise, counsel, purpose, devise, plan."[5] The repeated usage of the word *counsel* is for decision making or to accomplish a goal. For instance, when Absalom conspired to take the kingdom away from his father and sought counsel, Ahithophel proposed a plan to pursue David, smite him, and then bring those who had followed David back to Absalom. However, when Absalom consulted Hushai about the plan, Hushai said, "The counsel that Ahithophel hath given is not good at this time." Hushai then proposed another plan by which Absalom, instead, would be defeated (2 Samuel 17).

Counsel had to do with plans, guidance, and advice. Psalm 1:1 says, "Blessed is the man that walketh not in the counsel of the ungodly." That is, do not follow the advice, guidance, or plans of the ungodly. Psalm 2:2 gives another example of counsel: "The kings of the earth set themselves, and the rulers take counsel together, against the Lord, and against his anointed." Here a group is devising a plan in opposition to God.

If one compares the actual, contextual use of the word *counsel*, as well as the words *counsels* and *counselled*, one will see a great contrast between the biblical use of those words and the current biblical counselors who counsel people in their daily problems of living, habitual sins, emotional-behavioral problems, or any other such terms one might use. While there may be times when biblical counselors devise plans, propose a course of action, and give advice, the current practice of biblical counseling contains elements that go beyond the biblical use of the word *counsel*.

The most often misused example to establish biblical counseling is found in Exodus 18:13-26. The passage begins with a picture of Moses as he "sat to judge the people" and as "the people stood by Moses from the morning unto the evening." Moses' father-in-law, Jethro, asked Moses why that was happening and Moses answered:

> Because the people come unto me to inquire of God: When they have a matter, they come unto me; and I judge between one and another, and I do make them know the statutes of God, and his laws (Exodus 18:15-16).

In other words, Moses was judging according to the law of God. The word *counsel* is not even used to describe what Moses was doing. The word *counsel* is not used until Jethro is ready to give advice and present a plan to Moses, when Jethro said to Moses: "Hearken now unto my voice, I will give thee counsel." Jethro then presented a plan for Moses to teach the ordinances of God to the people and to:

> . . . provide out of all the people able men, such as fear God, men of truth, hating covetousness; and place such over them, to be rulers of thousands, and rulers of hundreds, rulers of fifties, and rulers of tens: And let them judge the people at all seasons: and it shall be, that every great matter they shall bring unto thee, but every small matter they

shall judge: so shall it be easier for thyself, and they shall bear the burden with thee (Exodus 18:21,22).

One commentary says the following about Moses:

> Having been employed to redeem Israel out of the house of bondage, herein he is a further type of Christ, that he is employed as a lawgiver and a judge among them. (1) He was to answer enquiries, and to explain the laws of God that were already given them, concerning the Sabbath, the manna, &c., beside the laws of nature, relating both to piety and equity, *v* 15. Moses made them *know the statutes of God and his laws, v.* 16. His business was, not to make laws, but to make known God's laws; his place was but that of a servant. (2) He was to decide controversies, judging between a man and his fellow, *v* 16. And, if the people were as quarrelsome one with another as they were with God, no doubt he had a great many causes brought before him.[6]

It must also be remembered that this incident preceded Mt. Sinai and the receiving of the Ten Commandments. Moses was judging the people. He was resolving controversies when disagreements occurred. He was not counseling problems of living like a contemporary biblical counselor, but was judging according to the "ordinances and laws."

While judging according to the "ordinances and laws" may be included in biblical counseling, there is a great difference between what Moses was doing and what present-day biblical counselors generally do. Examples of some of the differences will be seen in later chapters, which describe what goes on in biblical counseling.

In their eagerness to find what they do in Scripture, those who refer to themselves as "biblical counselors" turn judges into counselors, who follow a pattern that more resembles psychological counseling than judging by God's laws and ordinances. In our own eagerness for counseling according to the Word of God, we used Jethro's counsel to Moses to encourage pastors to share the burden of personal counsel with members of the body. We continue to believe the principle of sharing the burden applies, but we now conclude that the story of Jethro's advice to Moses is misapplied as a justification for the methodology of what is currently called "biblical counseling."

New Testament "Counsel"

In the New Testament, there are three words used in translation that seem to relate to the currently used terms in counseling. They are *counsel*, *counsellor*, and *counsels*. One of these words (*counsellor*) has to do with the person or persons giving the counsel. The remaining two have to do with what is counseled. Nevertheless, there is no example of biblical counseling as it is practiced in the church today. The word *counsel* is used 19 times in the New Testament. If one looks under the

word *counsel* in a concordance and then reads this
New Testament word in the context of the verses
listed, it will hardly be necessary to look in the
Greek dictionary to understand the meaning.

In many instances the word *counsel* is used to
describe the actions of those who opposed Jesus
and His disciples. For instance, Matthew 27:1
says, "When the morning was come, all the chief
priests and elders of the people took counsel
against Jesus to put him to death." The word
translated *counsel* in that and similar passages
refers to the idea of consulting together.

In contrast to the wicked counsel engaged in by
the enemies of Christ is the counsel of God, such as
in Ephesians 1:11, which speaks of believers "being
predestinated according to the purpose of him who
worketh all things after the counsel of his own
will." The word translated *counsel* in that passage
is *boule*, which means purpose, will, decision, resolution, counsel, or advice. The same word is used in
Acts 20:27, when Paul says, "For I have not
shunned to declare unto you all the counsel of
God." Indeed some biblical counselors will declare
much counsel of God in the process of their counseling, and that is what should go on in ministries
among believers. Yet, again, that is only part of
what occurs in contemporary biblical counseling.
The contemporary use of *counsel* in reference to
biblical counseling involves only distantly and tan-
gentially the meanings of the words used in the
New Testament.

The word *counsellor* is used three times in the
New Testament. Two of the times are used to

describe Joseph of Arimathaea and refer to his position as a member of the Jewish Sanhedrin. The other verse is Romans 11:34: "For who hath known the mind of the Lord? or who hath been his counsellor?" In other words, who would be so arrogant as to think he could advise God?

The only other word used is *counsels*, which is used only once, in 1 Corinthians 4:5: "Therefore judge nothing before the time, until the Lord come, who both will bring to light the hidden things of darkness, and will make manifest the counsels of the hearts: and then shall every man have praise of God." It is simply the plural of *boule*, which means purpose, will, decision, resolution, counsel, or advice. In this context *counsels* would refer to inner advising, planning, and directing within the heart of man. It certainly is not equivalent to the practice of biblical counseling in the twentieth century.

Obviously the New Testament use of the words translated as *counsel*, *counsellor*, and *counsels* do have shades of meaning in the Greek. However, in no instance does the use of those words justify what is currently called "biblical counseling."

We are not saying that these are the only words and examples associated with counseling in the Old and New Testaments. What we are saying is that there is no counseling found in the Bible as it is presently conducted by those who call themselves biblical counselors. One cannot use the definition of the above words to defend the practice of contemporary biblical counseling.

Neither the Old nor the New Testament has an equivalent word for *counselee*. In fact, the English word *counselee* did not show up in a dictionary until 1934. The definition of *counselee* in the *Oxford English Dictionary* is "One who receives professional counselling." No wonder it is nowhere in the Bible. Psychological counseling created the need for a word to designate those receiving "professional counseling." Yet biblical counselors faithfully call their recipients "counselees."

New Testament Gifts and Callings

Where is the office of counselor in the New Testament? Is there a specific calling of counselor as there is for evangelists, pastors and teachers? Are there specific offices as there are for elders and deacons? Why is the position of counselor absent, for instance, in Ephesians 4, which speaks of Christ's gifts to the church:

> And he gave some, apostles; and some, prophets; and some, evangelists; and some, pastors and teachers; For the perfecting of the saints, for the work of the ministry, for the edifying of the body of Christ: Till we all come in the unity of the faith, and of the knowledge of the Son of God, unto a perfect man, unto the measure of the stature of the fulness of Christ: That we henceforth be no more children, tossed to and fro, and carried about with every wind of doctrine, by the sleight of men, and cunning craftiness, whereby they lie in wait to deceive; But speaking the truth in love, may grow up into him in all things, which is the head, even

Christ: From whom the whole body fitly joined together and compacted by that which every joint supplieth, according to the effectual working in the measure of every part, maketh increase of the body unto the edifying of itself in love (Ephesians 4:11-16).

Everything necessary is accomplished through these gifts of ministry. With the great emphasis on counseling today, it is amazing that "counselor" is not in the list. Through the apostles, prophets, evangelists, pastors and teachers, the saints would be perfected. They would be equipped to do the "work of the ministry," they would be built up, they would attain unity based on their common faith in the Lord Jesus Christ, they would increase in their knowledge of Christ, and they would be complete in Him. Moreover, through those gifts of ministry, they would be so established in truth that they would not be deceived.

Besides the gifts of ministry is a body "fitly joined together and compacted by that which every joint supplieth, according to the effectual working in the measure of every part, maketh increase of the body unto the edifying of itself in love." Here is where the one-to-one ministry occurs. The one another edifying, encouraging, and supplying what is needed—the mutual caring and giving and loving—occurring as naturally as the different parts of the human body work together for health and well-being. Here there is no one-up-one-down relationship of counselor and "counselee." Instead there are apostles, prophets, evangelists, pastors, and teachers; and there is the mutual care, encouragement, and edification of all members of the body of Christ. Counsel may be given and received, but the real position of counselor is reserved for the Holy Spirit, who indwells every believer, who sees into the inner man, who applies the Word and makes it effectual in the believer, and then who enables the believer to glorify God through love and obedience.

It has been said by some, and we find that we agree, that those who take the position of counselor in someone else's life may be usurping the role of the Holy Spirit. Believers are called to comfort (1 Thessalonians 5:11), instruct (2 Timothy 2:24-26), edify (Romans 14:19), admonish (Romans 15:14), forgive (Ephesians 4:32), and restore (Galatians 6:1) one another. However, the only one who can see inside a person, and therefore be his real counselor, is the Lord Himself.

Rather than emphasizing counseling, the Scriptures emphasize teaching. For instance, Paul wrote to Timothy: "And the things that thou hast heard of me among many witnesses, the same commit thou to faithful men, who shall be able to teach others also" (2 Timothy 2:2). The older women were to teach the younger women: "To be discreet, chaste, keepers at home, good, obedient to their own husbands, that the word of God be not blasphemed" (Titus 2:5).

Some biblical counselors claim that they are simply teachers or that they are simply discipling other believers. If that is the case, why do they call themselves "counselors" and why do they follow the format of worldly counseling? While we see instances of teaching in Scripture, such instances do not resemble the process of counseling as it is practiced today, with weekly appointments and the exchange of money.

The word translated *teachers* is *didaskalos*. If teaching is what they do why not call it "biblical teaching" instead of "biblical counseling"? By picking up the word *counselor*, the rest of the baggage often comes along. And, counseling is the big attraction. That's where the prestige is in Christendom today. Counselors are often held in higher regard than pastors both inside and outside the church. The desire is for an expert in understanding human problems and how to deal with them. The assumption is that the trained counselor has special knowledge. The unspoken implication is that the pastor does not.

The special knowledge people seem to be looking for has to do with the soul itself, rather than external behavior. Even now among biblical counselors there are those who deal primarily with behavior and those who attempt to understand the motivations of the heart. There are those who look for the answers to people's problems in their past and in their "unconscious." There are those who believe Christians can be demon controlled and claim expertise at exorcism. And, there are those who counsel according to the four temperaments and their varied offshoots. The notions and nuances of biblical counseling range from incorporating aspects of secular counseling to engaging in unbiblical supernatural experimentation. Just as there are numerous different forms of psychological therapy with individual therapists practicing their own combination, so too with biblical counseling. While some have attempted to control the field through certificates, diplomas, degrees, and organizations, there is no single model or method of biblical counseling. Each counselor uses the Bible according to some combination of personal experience, secular theories, biblical doctrines, and "common sense." The best that can be said for biblical counseling is that there is the possibility that biblical counselors are more biblical than Christian psychologists.

While those who call themselves "biblical counselors" may be operating according to Scripture to some degree, they do so not within a position delineated in Scripture, because the New Testament does not present the position of the contemporary counselor. If they do minister biblically to another believer, they do so simply as a fellow believer or within ordained ministries presented in Scripture, such as an evangelist, pastor, teacher, elder, or deacon.

The replacement for psychological counseling is not biblical counseling. It is ministering the Word of God to one another in love, patience, and forbearance. It is believers being equipped through the apostles, prophets, evangelists, pastors, and teachers. Moreover, the Lord Himself eliminates the need for a psychologist or biblical counselor.

Our society places great value on the position of counselor, probably even higher than that of pastor, evangelist, or teacher. If the common name for a psychotherapist were "advisor" and the activity were called "advising," those would probably be the very words adopted by the church. Instead of "biblical counselors," there would be "biblical advisors" doing "biblical advising." If those terms sound dull and flat, it's because the powerful symbol is *counselor*, not *advisor*. An example of the centrality of biblical counseling over and above normal pastoral practice can be seen in the name change from *The Journal of Pastoral Practice* to *The Journal of Biblical Counseling*.

Christians need to move away from using the designations "biblical counseling" and "biblical counselor." The words *counseling* and *counselor* have become powerful symbols and suffer the same shortcomings within the church as they do outside the church. Because the terms *counsel* (verb form), *counselor*, *counselee*, and *counseling* have such strong roots, meanings, and ties to psychotherapy, we suggest replacing them. Possible changes are:

counsel	minister, evangelize, teach, pastor, disciple, come alongside, advise, encourage, admonish, exhort
counselor	minister, evangelist, teacher, pastor, fellow believer, elder, sister, brother
counselee	fellow believer, sister, brother, (or if not a believer, possible convert), person, individual
counseling	ministering, pastoring, evangelizing, teaching, discipling, encouraging, exhorting, admonishing, advising

A measure of the maturity of believers and evidence of their separation from the world will be the disappearance of those labels from their ministry. **We encourage biblical counsel to be given through the ministries of the church and through mutual care, one to another in the body of Christ.** However, we are concerned about biblical counseling separated from those ministries ordained by God. If the church had been teaching sound doctrine, pursuing the ministries and gifts designated in Scripture, and helping individuals to grow in the fruit of the Spirit, psychological counseling would have never attracted Christians, and biblical counseling would never have become a separate ministry either in or out of the church.

4

The Onerous Ones

Counseling is at the forefront of twentieth-century Christianity. Christian growth is equated with sound "mental health," and discipleship is equated with counseling. What happens in psychological counseling? What generally happens in biblical counseling? What similarities are there between psychological and biblical counseling? How should the church minister to individuals suffering from problems of living?

Some of the similarities between psychological counseling (psychotherapy) and biblical counseling are general matters of human relationship. (1) Conversation is used in an effort to help people overcome problems of living and thereby live more satisfying and productive lives. (2) Underlying the conversation are reasons as to why people are the way they are and how they change. (3) A major factor in change is the interpersonal relationship between the helper and the person seeking help.

These elements of human interaction existed long before the birth of Christ and millennia before the beginning of psychological counseling. They can be seen throughout the Bible. That is one of the reasons Christians have been willing to embrace psychology. They see the similarities, but not the grave differences.

Two people speak. One speaks the oracles of God; the other speaks from the kingdom of darkness. Are they the same just because both are speaking? Two people listen to a description of a dream. One says only God can interpret dreams, but the other employs the theories of such men as Freud and Jung. Will they give the same answer? Two people will describe the inner man and seek to explain why people act the way they do. One will use only the Bible, but the other will add notions from secular psychology. Two people will demonstrate care and concern in their interactions. One speaks the truth in love, but the other presents the wisdom of men in a caring and compassionate manner. Are they the same? While the above activities seem similar on the surface, they come from opposite sources and lead in opposite directions.

Another group of similarities between psychotherapy and biblical counseling did not exist from the beginning. They are practices that were developed by psychological practitioners and then imitated by biblical counselors. The following elements of psychological counseling are examples of the kinds of practices that biblical counseling has emulated with no biblical justification. Although this chapter is primarily directed at biblical counseling ministries that are separated from the church, much of it applies to biblical counseling ministries inside the church.

One to One

The first element of psychotherapy is that of a one-to-one relationship. Yes, therapists do meet with couples and some meet with whole families. However, the main form of therapy is still one-to-one. And, regardless of how many are in the room with the therapist, it still provides a setting that is synthetic. It is synthetic in that the therapist does not interact with the individual or with the family members outside the therapeutic setting, unless another artificial situation, such as group therapy, is added to the treatment. The therapist has no responsibility for the individual before or after the counseling session, unless phone calls are allowed as part of the treatment or in case of "emergency."

This error of an artificial, limited, one-to-one relationship is emulated by many in biblical counseling, especially when provided outside the church. Apart from the church body, there is little opportunity to interact with a "counselee" as a fellow believer, in the context of mutual care and concern. Within the church body everyone has an opportunity to minister one to another. If the church operates according to New Testament principles, it will provide opportunities to help one another in a variety of ways. The helping examples are numerous and are as simple as providing food or as important as helping with finances. This does not happen in psychotherapy, and it does not happen in biblical counseling offices outside a church.

Besides lacking the advantages of the various helps available within the church body, a counselor in a biblical counseling center separate from a church does not know the person being counseled apart from what is learned through a cold and impersonal, data collecting, intake form and through what is said during the counseling sessions. Perhaps that is why so many centers attempt to speed up the process of getting to know the person through administering various personality tests and inventories. Even though such personality tests are too subjective to give valid results, numerous biblical counselors administer the tests and trust the inaccurate snapshot of the person to be counseled. Not only is this an additional artificial technique; such tests put people into arbitrary, unbiblical categories that fail to give accurate, specific knowledge about the individual.

Without the church context, the counselor is limited to superficial means of knowing that person. Furthermore, unless he checks everything the person being counseled tells him, the counselor's perception may be limited to the information the person chooses to reveal about himself during counseling.

One very serious concern in the artificial one-to-one counseling relationship has to do with gender and temptation. Over the years most therapists have been men and most patients and clients have been women. In fact, if all women discontinued therapy and counseling, the entire system would collapse. In both psychological and biblical counseling, the predominant relationship is a man counseling a woman. Both psychological therapists and biblical counselors have admitted inappropriate sexual contact (sexual sin). Even when outward sin is not committed, the counselor may usurp the husband's role of authority and leadership. The woman may become more devoted to the therapist than to her own husband. She might compare the counselor's one session of attentiveness, concern, and compassion with an entire week of living with a husband who is less than perfect. But, as more women are entering the psychotherapeutic ranks, more women are counseling men. This is an entirely unbiblical position for a woman, who is not "to teach, nor to usurp authority over the man" (1 Timothy 2:12).

There is also an important matter of church leadership responsibilities, which include biblical teaching, worship, and, if necessary, biblical discipline. None of these occur in biblical counseling separated from the church. A separate ministry cannot hold an individual responsible through discipline. A separate ministry cannot remove a person from fellowship for the purpose of restoration. Furthermore, a separate counseling center may teach different doctrines from those of the individual's own church. Therefore, the individual who is experiencing problems of living needs the church and its ministries, not a separate counseling office away from the church.

Those who minister in the body of Christ are to be under the authority and leadership of the local church, whether they are ordained as pastor, teacher, or elder, or whether they are simply members of the body involved in mutual care. Within the context of the church there is both leadership and accountability. However, in separate counseling centers, church leadership is absent. Presumably anyone can open a so-called biblical counseling office and sell his services to fellow believers in the same way professional psychotherapists open offices apart from the authority and leadership of a church. Then, when Christians buy counseling services from these outside agencies, they do so without the leadership, protection, and accountability of a body of believers organized to perform the work of the ministry according to Ephesians 4:11-16.

One Day a Week

"See you once a week but never outside the office if I can help it" is a definite limitation in psychotherapy. One psychotherapist points out the paradox of the therapeutic relationship. He says that while the relationship is "one of the most intimate in human life . . . the therapist . . . has no interest in seeing the patient outside the office."[1] Therapists generally avoid social contacts with their clients, and clients cannot see the therapist outside this one day a week, unless additional appointments are made.

The one-to-one error is compounded by the one-day-a-week error. That error is one of a relationship limited to only one day a week and only more often by appointment. Personal phone calls and attempts to arrange more frequent contact other than at the office are discouraged, if not avoided all together.

This error is replicated in biblical counseling separated from the church. The greater the distance to the biblical counseling office, the less likely additional appointments will be made and the less likely outside-the-office contacts will ever occur.

In a church, the possibilities for personal contact and communication by phone are readily available. The possibilities are only limited by the number of individuals available. There is no barrier as in psychotherapy and biblical counseling separated from the church. Christians can choose when and how often to meet together for personal ministry. In the body of Christ this can be done freely without the time constraints of professional counseling

One Hour

In addition to the one-to-one and one-day-a-week errors in psychotherapy, there is the fifty-minute hour limitation. Why a fifty-minute hour? The fifty-minute hour is a device that meets the needs of the psychotherapist to regulate the flow of clients for convenience and income. The length of time benefits the counselor, not the client.

Normal relationships sometimes work on time schedules, but more often they do not. However, the psychotherapeutic relationship is governed by the clock. If the client is late, he loses time from the already reduced hour. The positive aspects of the client meeting the time restraints of the system are primarily to the advantage of the therapist, who must see a number of clients throughout the day. One must recognize that such restrictions do not lend themselves to developing caring relationships. The mark on the calendar and the hand on the clock must be followed, even if it means an interruption and "next please."

Here is another error that biblical counseling has inherited from its sibling psychotherapy. In a situation in which one Christian is ministering to another, time can be flexible. One does not turn on and off a relationship by the hand on the clock. Time is a precious gift by which we can demonstrate Christian love. Just giving time is a way of saying, "I care about you." And, the number of hours available through many members in a church supersedes what is available or affordable in psychotherapy. The church is a place that is not bound by the one-to-one, one-day-a-week, one-hour relationships of psychotherapy and of many biblical counseling centers.

One Week after Another

One-to-one, one-day-a-week and one-hour errors of psychotherapy and biblical counseling are compounded by one week after another. Sigmund Freud began what resulted in the psychotherapy craze that exists today. Freud's system, called psychoanalysis, used to be almost universally considered the most effective therapy. Undergoing psychoanalysis generally involved three to five sessions per week over a period of three to five years. Thus the pattern was set for long-term therapy.

Since the time of Freud numerous forms of psychotherapy have been developed. Yet, many therapists continue to retain clients over extended periods of time. Many attempt to hold individuals as long as they possibly can for the ostensible reason that there is still improvement to be made. Yet there is the financial side as well. We have seen workshops and professional psychotherapy magazines advertise both how to attract and how to retain clients. The longer one keeps a client the more certain is the psychotherapist's income.

Recently, however, both the length and type of treatment in psychoanalysis has come under attack. Some of the most vocal critics have been Adolf Grunbaum, Jeffrey Masson, Thomas Szasz, E. Fuller Torrey, and Garth Wood, along with numerous others. We have noted these criticisms of psychoanalysis in our other writings. Along with the valid concerns about psychoanalysis has come concern about all forms of long-term therapy.

Contrary to the research and like secular psychotherapists, many biblical counselors keep individuals week after week, month after month, and some of them even year after year. For many, counseling becomes a way of life. We have often

heard biblical counselors speak of counseling individuals for months and years. When Nathan
confronted David with his sin, Nathan did not have
a long-term counseling plan for David. When one
truly hears from God, as Nathan did, and when one
truly confesses and repents of his sin, as David did,
there's no need for another appointment.

Long-term counseling relationships also deterio-
rate into dependency relationships. People in counseling often become dependent on their counselors
rather than on the Lord. Biblical ministry should
always lead in the direction of dependency on the
Lord Himself. The more dependent a person is on
the Lord, the less dependent he will be on a counselor and the less inclined he will be to pursue
long-term counseling.

In a church where the ministries are function-
ing and the gifts are operating, long-term formal
biblical counseling relationships are entirely
unnecessary. A believer may need some personal,
short-term (once or twice) counsel as to what to do
in a particular situation. The ongoing ministries of
the church and the mutual care and encouragement of fellow believers should be there to assist
the Christian in his ongoing walk with the Lord.
Church leaders and lay people ministering biblically to one another preempt a one-to-one, one-day-
a-week, one-hour, one-week-after-another
relationship that is often dictated by a counseling
ministry separated from the church.

One Fixed Price

The one-to-one, one-day-a-week, one-hour, one-week-after-another errors are almost eclipsed by one fixed price. The establishing, billing and collecting of fees constitute a significant part of psychotherapy. Because of salaries and bills to be paid, the one fixed price becomes a necessity that limits the relationship. Generosity is a mark of genuine friendship. The only possibility for such generosity within the psychotherapeutic relationship might be a discount for a long term or poor client. These, however, are the exceptions rather than the rule. Generally, if one cannot pay his bill, the relationship is over. The mark in the checkbook must match the mark in the appointment book.

As with most professionals, time and money are two very important ingredients to psychotherapists. To make a professional income, he must schedule and adhere to the fifty-minute hour. The fifty-minute hour regulates the number of clients per day, week and month, which, in turn, produces the necessary dollars per day, week and month. A psychotherapist must fill enough fifty-minute hours to make a desirable income. Thus, psychotherapy is a business that tends to revolve around time and money, rather than around people and their concerns.

We say categorically that any biblical counseling ministry that charges a price is unbiblical. Yes, "the labourer is worthy of his hire" (Luke 10:7), and "the labourer is worthy of his reward" (1 Timothy 5:18). Paul even argued that as he had sown spiritual things, should he not also

reap carnal things (1 Corinthians 9:11). Nevertheless, he also said: "What is my reward then? Verily
that, when I preach the gospel, I may make the
gospel of Christ without charge, that I abuse not
my power in the gospel" (1 Corinthians 9:18). Peter
wrote to the elders: "Feed the flock of God which is
among you, taking the oversight thereof, not by
constraint, but willingly; not for filthy lucre, but of
a ready mind" (1 Peter 5:2).

Whether one agrees with biblical counseling or
not, it is a ministry. It is designed to minister the
Word of God empowered by the Holy Spirit by one
who knows Christ to one who will receive it. It is
unbiblical to charge for such a ministry. There is no
example in Scripture to charge a fee for ministering the Word of God by the grace of God to a
brother or sister in Christ. Someone might protest
that a minister is paid a salary. But that is a false
analogy. The true analogy would be charging someone a fee to attend church. We hope no one would
even think of doing such a thing!

This pay for service makes any biblical counseling grossly unbiblical. Imagine someone going to a
biblical counseling center for ministry concerning a
life issue? Let's say that the conversation and
direction are biblical. Can you imagine at the end a
prayer and Amen, and then a request to pay by
cash, check or credit card? Would Paul or the disciples have done such a thing? Absolutely not!

Love is hardly a relationship that can be bought
with money. Jesus gave freely of His life and love,
and He asks us to do the same. "Love one another,
as I have loved you"(John 15:12). A person seeking

biblical help for problems of living should be given biblical love, friendship and guidance. The body of believers can and should offer this type of caring without basing the relationship on time and money. Christian counsel is a form of body ministry in which a relationship is not based on the need to make an income; it is a ministry that cannot be bought.

With salaries that need to be paid and overhead expenses, independent counseling centers would no doubt cease to exist without a sizable fee for service. However, it would be better to cease and become biblical than to survive and be unbiblical. A fixed price charge for ministry is not in the Bible; it comes from the secular world of psychotherapy and is one more reason to reject what is now known as "biblical counseling."

One Right after Another

One person right after another comes into the one-to-one, one-day-a-week, one-hour, one-week-after-another, one-fixed-price relationship. Since time and money are crucial to the professional psychotherapist, the regular process in a therapist's office is one person right after another, with clients going in and out of the office like factory workers on various shifts at an assembly plant. This is not necessarily a criticism of the treatment they receive once they arrive and have entered their time slot. It is simply a picture of a process that works by the clock. Clients know very well that they have been preceded by others and will be followed by more.

Time and money require numbers of clients. No one has set a limit on how many clients a day or week a therapist should ideally see. The American Medical Association estimates that the average psychiatrist has about 51 client visits weekly.[2] One psychotherapist (a professing Christian) brags about seeing forty-five people every week.[3] Evidently therapists assume that numbers don't matter. The diminishing point of return is an individual affair. Thus, no one sets a limit on numbers, and time and money become the final determinants.

Practicing therapy eight hours a day, five days a week, with large numbers of people always has and always will lead to superficial relationships lacking genuine compassion. It seems axiomatic that the greater the variety and numbers of people, the less effective we become. No amount of training, techniques, or licenses will overcome the obstacle of numbers.

The business of biblical counseling, like psychotherapy, necessitates a one-right-after-another flow of individuals. And most often one woman after another. There is no biblical example for this. No, not even the example of Moses, as indicated earlier.

There is a real contrast between a paid listener who is driven by financial necessity to fill a calendar of appointments with forty to fifty persons per week and a body of believers who freely minister to one another without the necessity to see large numbers of people by appointment for the sake of income.

One Up/One Down

A very serious onerous One is the one-up/one-down relationship in both psychological and biblical counseling. The psychologist is considered the expert, the authority with special knowledge and wisdom. This is an artificial hierarchy of the expert over the needy one. The psychologist as seer is not supported by the research, as we have demonstrated elsewhere.[4] It has an authoritative power invested by society. In fact, the world has elevated the psychotherapist to the place of priest.

When the Lord calls a believer to minister counsel to another believer, there is to be meekness and humility, not a demonstration of expertise or a show of superiority. Paul says:

> Brethren, if a man be overtaken in a fault, ye which are spiritual, restore such an one in the spirit of meekness; considering thyself, lest thou also be tempted (Galatians 6:1).

Yes, believers are called to minister to one another through the gifts of ministry and as fellow believers encouraging one another in the faith, but even those in leadership stand on an equal plain at the foot of the cross, because it is the Lord who truly accomplishes the restoration and sanctification of the believer.

Conclusion

The therapeutic situation is filled with onerous Ones: a one-to-one relationship, one day a week, one fifty-minute hour, one week after another, one fixed price, and one right after another in a one-up/one-down relationship. The Ones add up to one great advantage for the therapist, but one great limitation for a real relationship for the client. In true, natural relationships, persons are sometimes alone together and sometimes with others; they sometimes do things on a fixed schedule and some-times spontaneously; sometimes one pays and sometimes the other pays. Activities that happen naturally with friends rarely or almost never hap-pen in psychotherapy. Normally, a rate is set and a service provided, but don't expect anything beyond what you pay for.

While it is true that therapists care for and love some of their clients, it is also true that they hate others. Just as the personality characteristics of the therapist affect the client, the client's personal-ity characteristics affect the therapist. Love is an important ingredient in the success of therapy, and the effects the client and therapist have on one another will increase or decrease the possibility of improvement. Add to this the lack of real involve-ment implied by the discovery of one researcher, who "found that 50 percent of clinical psychologists no longer believed in what they were doing and wished they had chosen another profession."[5]

Because of the limitations we have just reviewed, the usual therapeutic situation provides little or no opportunity for the deeper aspects of a healing relationship. A limited (one to one), timed (50 minutes), fixed (one day a week), continuous (one week after another), paid (one fixed price), routine (one right after another), unequal (one-up/one-down) relationship leaves little room for depth or creativity. Although an occasional relationship under these circumstances may have depth, most are generally superficial or absent of love. But, some people are so hard up for love that even the most superficial looks good. The client often perceives any attention at all to be worthwhile and valuable.

It has been said that a psychotherapist is merely a paid friend, and a highly paid friend at that. Loneliness is a common affliction in America. Many people do not have real friends. However, for those who have no friends, the psychotherapeutic rent-a-friend may seem better than no one at all. At its best psychotherapy is rent-a-friend, but usually it's rent-a-service.

True friends are involved in one another's lives. A "paid friend" who has "one right after another" can't really become involved in each client's life. Personal involvement is a demand that exceeds the onerous Ones. These onerous Ones make psychotherapy look shallow and artificial when compared with the reality of true caring.

Unfortunately biblical counseling is too often conducted with the same onerous Ones operating. Christians are called into a family love relationship: "Be kindly affectioned one to another with brotherly love" (Romans 12:10). Thus, in ministering to one another, believers give love freely. A true friend in Christ is of far greater value than a paid psychotherapist or a paid biblical counselor, not only because the love is freely given, but also because the love is biblically given in a biblical setting: the body of Christ.

All biblical counseling is vulnerable to the criticisms in this chapter. Particularly vulnerable are those counseling ministries that operate separately from the local church. **A step forward for those in the biblical counseling movement would be to discontinue all biblical counseling centers that operate outside a church.**

An Example

An example of a biblical counseling service separated from the church is the Christian Counseling and Educational Foundation (CCEF). CCEF is flawed with all of the errors of psychological counseling discussed in this chapter. One example of their flagrant flaws is found in *The Journal of Biblical Counseling*, which is published by CCEF. In an article written by Leslie Vernick, she talks about counseling a couple having marital problems. In the process, Vernick (a woman) works theologically and authoritatively with both the husband and wife. During one session, it appears that Vernick is working exclusively with the husband.[6] Our further concern with this is that the counseling setting is separated from a church and a fee is involved.

This leads us to a second example of their flagrant flaws, which is that of one fixed price. CCEF reported an income in 1992-93 of almost one-half million dollars from counseling fees alone![7] In the same publication, CCEF reports that they received almost a quarter of a million dollars in educational income. While the charge for educational seminars is not the subject of this book, we note it because of a letter we received advertising a CCEF seminar at a church. The pastor of the church advertised the weekend seminar by stating, "Total cost of the seminar is $6000." The pastor explains, "If we have twenty people attending, the cost will be $300. If thirty, the cost will be $200."[8]

The total annual revenue reported by CCEF for 1992-93 is over one million dollars. While our immediate concern is the one-fixed-price issue, we note their total income to reveal that a biblical counseling center that charges fees for counseling can be a big business. Is that what Paul meant when he spoke of the ministries given to the church?

> For the perfecting of the saints, for the work of the ministry, for the edifying of the body of Christ: Till we all come in the unity of the faith, and of the knowledge of the Son of God, unto a perfect man, unto the measure of the stature of the fulness of Christ: That we henceforth be no more children, tossed to and fro, and carried about with every wind of doctrine, by the sleight of men, and cunning craftiness, whereby they lie in wait to deceive; But speaking the truth in love, may grow up into him in all things, which is the head, even Christ: From whom the whole body fitly joined together and compacted by that which every joint supplieth, according to the effectual working in the measure of

every part, maketh increase of the body unto the edifying of itself in love (Ephesians 4:12-16).

5

Biblical Counseling Compromise

Most Christian counselors are not content to rely solely on the Word of God and the work of the Holy Spirit in their counseling. Many have gleaned notions from secular theorists. They call their attempt to wed psychological theories with the Bible *integration*. Their goal is to integrate or amalgamate the truth of Scripture with the so-called truth of psychology to produce a hybrid that is superior to the truth of each. They make the faulty assumption that psychological "truth" is scientific truth and build on a faulty understanding of "all truth is God's truth." This slogan appears to be the alpha and omega of the amalgamationists.

Dr. Gary Collins, a popular psychologist and psychologizer of Christianity and the author and editor of more than twenty books, says in his book *Psychology and Theology: Prospects for Integration*:

> . . . there will be no conflict or contradiction between truth as revealed in the Bible (studied by Bible scholars and theologians), and truth as revealed in nature (studied by scientists, including psychologists and other scholars).[1]

That is his basis for integrating psychology and theology. However, he does not define integration or what brands of psychology and theology he hopes to integrate.

Dr. John Carter and Dr. Bruce Narramore, both of Rosemead Graduate School of Psychology, have written a book titled *The Integration of Psychology and Theology*.[2] Carter and Narramore refer to and repeat, "All truth is God's truth." This incantation—the abracadabra of integrationists—is sprinkled throughout their book and throughout the writings of others who espouse the amalgamationists' position. Such books repeatedly state, but cannot support, the "all truth is God's truth" platitude. They talk about it but cannot demonstrate the connection between "all truth is God's truth" and so-called psychological truth. The lack of uniformity in psychological theories and practices among those who preach integration should prove that theological-psychological amalgamania is in a sad state of confusion.

With 450 competing and often contradictory therapies[3] and over 10,000 not-always-compatible techniques, and with the lack of consistency among Christian therapists and their great variety of approaches, one has to conclude that the integrationists make what they call "God's truth" look more than just a little confused. When one reads what scientists and philosophers of science have said, one must conclude that this kind of psychology is not scientific. Therefore, even appealing to natural revelation will not do unless God's truth equals personal opinion. The use of psychotherapy in Christianity is not a testimony to science. It is a testimony to how much Christians can be deceived.

Biblical theology did without psychology for almost two thousand years. The prophets of the Old Testament, the disciples and apostles of the New Testament, and the saints right up to the present century did very well without psychology. Why would the church need the modern-day psychologizers now? How would a twentieth-century psychologist respond to Ezekiel seeing "a wheel in the middle of a wheel," or to Elijah hearing "a still small voice," or Isaiah seeing "the Lord sitting upon a throne, high and lifted up," or Peter and his vision of unclean things, or the man who was caught up to the third heaven?

To even hint that the often-conflicting "discoveries" of such unredeemed men as Freud, Jung, Adler, Rogers, etc., are God's truth is to undermine the very Word of God. The revealed Word of God does not need the support or the help of psychological pronouncements. The Word alone stands as the truth of God. That psychologists who call themselves Christian would even use such a phrase to justify their use of psychology indicates the direction and nature of their faith.

Psychotherapy is not science. It is not scientific theory. Psychotherapy rests upon the erroneous assumption that problems of thinking and living constitute illnesses or pathologies and, therefore, require cures by psychologically trained professionals. One writer very wisely pointed out that prevailing popular psychotherapeutic systems merely reflect the current culture.[4] The truths of Scripture are eternal. But, which psychological "truths" are eternal or even temporarily valid? It is unfortunate that Christians have followed the psychological way and its pseudosolutions to real problems.

Because of psychotherapy's nonstatus as a science and because it is nonsense as medicine, people who choose psychotherapy do so by faith. They believe the claims of psychotherapy rather than the research evidence. Psychotherapy falls short of the objectivity and testability of science. It is not a coherent science in principle or in theory, diagnosis, or treatment.

For years we have accused numerous individuals and institutions in the church of promoting psychoheresy. We now say that many who call themselves "biblical counselors" are guilty of the same. These biblical counselors depart from the fundamental truths of the Gospel by using the unproved and unscientific psychological opinions of men, rather than having complete confidence in the biblical truth of God. They have chosen to combine dregs from the broken cisterns of man-made ideas with the fresh springs of living water and thereby serve mixed drinks that poison the soul.

One response to the proliferation of the psychological way among Christians was to offer a biblical alternative with centers for biblical counseling and for training counselors. However, one of the most serious issues facing the biblical counseling movement today is the integration of psychology and the Bible. Though the intent of those who developed biblical counseling programs was to provide a biblical means of addressing problems of living, biblical counseling is often like the very system it seeks to replace. Many such counseling centers are afflicted with integration problems. It is our impression that the ones most open to the integration of psychological models and methods are those that function independently from a local church body. These are scattered across America and vary in their theology and in their use of psychology.

CCEF: One Example of Problems

In critiquing biblical counseling training, we have chosen to examine the Christian Counseling and Educational Foundation (CCEF) in Laverock, Pennsylvania, since it is one of the best known and most respected in the field. Other organizations are either somewhat related to CCEF, such as the National Association of Nouthetic Counselors (NANC) in Lafayette, Indiana, or they are similar, such as the Biblical Counseling Foundation (BCF) in Rancho Mirage, California.

The critique of CCEF, as an example of serious problems with the biblical counseling movement, will include brief background information, questionable endorsements, problems with the curriculum, invited integrationist speakers, and some of the writings and teachings of the director and three other staff members.

CCEF began in 1968 under the inspiration and leadership of Dr. Jay Adams, who is considered the founder of this movement. While Adams calls his method of biblical counseling "nouthetic counseling," as we speak in this book of the counseling at CCEF, we will refer to it under its more generic label, "biblical counseling."

Dr. John Bettler, cofounder of CCEF along with Adams, became the head of the organization in 1974. At that time Adams, who had been teaching at Westminster Theological Seminary in Philadelphia, moved to Georgia to pursue further writing on the subject of counseling. From that time until the present, CCEF has developed primarily under Bettler's leadership. CCEF has grown as an institution. Besides training counselors for degree programs at Westminster Theological Seminary, CCEF offers short-term certificate programs for pastors and other church workers and conducts workshops and week-long Summer Institutes.

Bettler describes CCEF this way:

> Ivy-covered walls surround many of the best schools in the Northeast. Since it takes time for ivy to grow, these institutions represent a long-standing tradition of solid

> scholarship and a community of serious academic reflection.
>
> Ivy covers the walls of CCEF; it has grown thick and lush over the last twenty-five years. CCEF also represents the best in counselor education. From all over the world people travel to our ivy-covered walls to learn how to counsel from men and women who take the Bible seriously, who have honed their skills through years of extensive counseling experience and communicate in an easy-to learn, quick-to-apply style.[5]

That is an apt description of how CCEF sees itself, not only in taking the Bible seriously, but in the "tradition of solid scholarship" and "serious academic reflection." In this chapter and the one following, we will look at how seriously they take the Bible and how interested they are in integration. This chapter is a summary of two critiques we wrote on CCEF.[6]

CCEF Endorsements

The most recent CCEF catalog includes endorsements by five individuals, who appear in past catalogs as well. The views these individuals have about biblical counseling must be compatible with those of CCEF, since their endorsements are in the catalog. One of the endorsers is Dr. Jerry Falwell, who is one of the strongest proponents of the integration of psychology and the Bible in the entire evangelical church. Under his leadership, Liberty University has developed a large program in psychology, precisely the kind that biblical counselors should oppose. In addition to the regular program, psychology is featured in its correspondence school (Liberty University School of LifeLong Learning) and in the Liberty Institute for Lay Counseling. The extreme integration position is found throughout Liberty University. Much of the teaching is purely psychological! As a natural consequence of Falwell's commitment to psychology, he also endorses Rapha Hospital Treatment Centers, which offer private psychiatric hospital treatment with a heavy dose of self-worth and a Christian veneer.

Information gathered from the five endorsers indicates that all five lack full confidence in the biblical way. For example, one of them refers individuals to licensed psychological professionals; another recommends books by psychologist James Dobson and uses materials based upon the writings of Dr. Elizabeth Kübler-Ross; and a third employs psychological tests with poor validity.[7]

In the CCEF catalog, endorser Dr. Joseph K. Newmann says:

> As a clinical psychologist, I had for several years functioned as a "secular priest" of humanism. When I became a Christian in 1979, I knew I needed to integrate my counseling training and experience with my newfound faith. God graciously led me to CCEF.[8]

Note the word *integrate,* and note what is being integrated: secular "counseling training and experience" and "my new found faith."

Announcement of the Diploma Program

A previous CCEF catalog includes a course titled "Scientific Psychology I" (CC43). Part of the description says:

> Along with reading the research articles, students take or review a variety of psychological tests. These tests include the MMPI, TJTA, Myers-Briggs, intelligence tests, projective tests and vocational tests. In addition to **potential personal benefits from such testing**, first-hand familiarity with these tests allows students to make informed judgments regarding the place of psychologist tests in biblical counseling.[9] (Emphasis added.)

What are the "personal benefits" of taking the MMPI, TJTA, and the Myers-Briggs tests? What is "the place of psychological tests in biblical counseling"? The Myers-Briggs Type Indicator is based upon Jungian psychology. There are serious problems with the use of such tests, regarding validity and the theories on which the tests are based.[10] A more recent catalog indicates that "Scientific Psychology I" (CC43) has been replaced by "Introduction to Psychological Assessment" (CC47). Thus CCEF continues to teach psychological testing in its curriculum.

Invited Integrationist Speakers at CCEF

Dr. Lawrence Crabb, who calls his blend of psychology and Christianity "biblical counseling,"[11] was an invited speaker at CCEF. The advertisement in the CCEF publication *Pulse* states:

> Dr. Larry Crabb will offer an intense two-day course on "Core Issues in Biblical Counseling."
>
> The course will focus on (but not be limited to) the operation of self-deception, how to develop a biblical understanding of problems which the Bible does not specifically address, and the role of community in change.[12]

Crabb was invited to speak again at CCEF. The CCEF advertisement says:

> "Methods for Change" will be the topic of Larry Crabb's upcoming seminar. According to Dr. Crabb, understanding people is only half the battle in counseling. You must also help them make significant changes in their life strategies. How to take these next steps will be the focus of Dr. Crabb's workshop.
>
> Malcom Osborn, CCEF's registrar, puts it this way: "Last year he gave us the theory. This year he'll show us how. Don't miss this critical next step."[13]

Yet, in his comments on Crabb in *Prophets of PsychoHeresy I*, Dr. Jay Adams says:

[Crabb] does not believe the Scriptures are sufficient to enable Christian counselors to counsel adequately. This fundamental flaw lies beneath all the other errors apparent in the system.

In conclusion Adams says:

In my opinion, I believe Crabb sincerely wants to be biblical and thinks that his system is. But so long as he continues to build his basic system out of pagan materials, according to the erroneous speculations of unsaved men, he will never achieve his goal. Painting such views in biblical hues does not transform them. To be biblical, the system itself, from the ground up, must be built of biblical materials according to God's plan. This Crabb has not yet done.[14]

Psychology professor Dr. Paul Vitz was also an invited speaker at CCEF. The advertisement in *Pulse* says:

CCEF is extremely pleased to announce that Dr. Vitz will offer a two-day seminar entitled, "Christianity and Psychology: An Insider's View."[15]

Four years earlier Vitz had written two articles for the *Journal of Psychology and Theology* titled "Christianity and Psychoanalysis (Parts One and Two): Jesus As The Anti-Oedipus."[16] Vitz contends that Jung, Freud, etc., were correct in their descriptions of human behavior, but that Jesus is the answer because "Jesus is the anti-Oedipus." In the book *The Christian Vision: Man in Society*, edited by Lynne Morris, Vitz says:

> And in the long run I believe it will be possible to "baptize" large portions of secular psychology; that is, to use what is valid in them, while removing their anti-Christian threat.[17]

If one reads Vitz's articles "Christianity and Psychoanalysis" (Parts One and Two) and the chapter in the above book, he will inescapably discover that Vitz is an integrationist. CCEF said they were "especially pleased to have him." It is also true that Fuller Seminary Graduate School of Psychology (integrationist) was pleased to have him speak there.

CCEF Staff Members

More serious than the external speakers' compromise with psychological theories and therapies are those of regular CCEF staff members. Here we will only consider the writing, speaking, and questionable memberships of four members: Dr. John Bettler, Dr. Ed Welch, Leslie Vernick and David Powlison.

Dr. John Bettler

Since Dr. John Bettler is in charge of CCEF, he must bear the final responsibility for its integrationist position. Bettler is a member of the North American Society of Adlerian Psychology (NASAP) and a clinical member of the American Association for Marriage and Family Therapy (AAMFT). These organizations are purely and simply psychologically oriented groups. The requirements for clinical membership in the AAMFT are extensive and cover four pages in its brochure. We question the wisdom of anyone who is committed to biblical counseling, instead of psychological counseling, being interested in belonging to those two organizations, meeting their requirements for membership, or even attending their conferences.

In a talk he gave at the 1991 NANC (National Association of Nouthetic Counselors) conference, Bettler mentioned his "tremendous appreciation for Larry Crabb."[18] (Crabb's "biblical counseling" includes psychological notions neither based on nor supported by Scripture.[19]) Bettler praised Crabb with the following words:

> You read the first 70 pages of *Understanding People* where Crabb puts forth his view of the sufficiency of Scripture and I doubt if there's anyone in this conference here who wouldn't subscribe to that. I mean it is excellent, excellent material! Crabb is upholding the Scripture as sufficient.[20]

Bettler also referred to *The Marriage Builder* as "one of the good books he [Crabb] wrote." Although Bettler does say there's a lot on which he disagrees with Crabb, one is left with Bettler's high praise of him.

We disagree with Bettler's appraisal of *Understanding People*, his "tremendous appreciation" for Crabb, and his recommendation of *The Marriage Builder*.[21] As we will show in the next chapter, there is at least a "recycled" Adlerian connection between Bettler and Crabb, which is one of the many reasons we recommend against what CCEF calls "recycling."

Dr. Edward Welch

Welch, a staff member of CCEF, is listed in the CCEF catalog as being both a member of the American Psychological Association (APA) and a licensed psychologist. Such affiliations represent more than a thread of compromise with the promoters of psychological counseling theories and therapies; they demonstrate a lack of full confidence in the biblical way. During a CCEF West Conference at Point Loma, California, Welch mentioned that he was favorably impressed with the work of C. G. Jung. Jung was an avowed occultist who admitted that he developed his theories under the influence of spirit guides.[22] Welch also said, "I appreciate lots of things that Larry Crabb has done."[23]

Leslie Vernick

In the Summer 1988 CCEF *Pulse*, a reference was made to a talk by CCEF staff member Leslie Vernick on counseling children. The article states: "One of the talks receiving the highest marks was Leslie Vernick's presentation on counseling children who were subject to abuse." It is obvious that Leslie Vernick is a very popular speaker among the CCEF staff and alumni, because she gave another talk on the same subject at the 1990 Alumni Conference. It was thought of so highly that it was excerpted for an article in the Summer 1990 *Pulse*. Vernick's article "When Sexually Abused Children Grow Up, What Do the Scriptures Say to Them?" demonstrates a great commitment to psychology and a lack of commitment to the Scripture for dealing with sins such as sexual abuse of children. Her article is contrary to Adams' book *The Language of Counseling*, in which he says:

> The prejudicial language of psychotherapeutic labeling is perhaps the most glaring example of language abuse that we must consider. And yet there are others, not quite so apparent, that, by reason of their subtlety, are all the more dangerous.[24]

Vernick's article errs in both categories by the use of "the prejudicial language of psychotherapeutic labeling" and the less apparent, but "all the more dangerous" use of psychological ideas amalgamated with or justified by Scripture. Vernick has misrepresented the research on sexual abuse of children, promoted her own personal psychological ideas, and perverted Scripture to prove her position.

Throughout the article Vernick does much psychologizing, which she attempts to support with what she regards as biblical evidence. However, her conclusions are not derived from Scripture. It is evident throughout that she obtained her ideas from the world and then attempted to support them with Scripture. Her article lacks any clear development of the biblical doctrine of depravity. And, she does not present a clear biblical answer to know God, trust Him, and particularly to obey Him. Vernick is primarily a psychological counselor who has mutilated Scripture to prove her psychological opinions. She has a Freudian orientation and psychological methodology and language.[25]

In the issue of *Pulse* that followed the one mentioned above, an announcement headline asks, "Does Your Childhood Abuse Still Hurt?" The description states:

> If you are a woman who is still suffering from the effects of childhood sexual or physical abuse, CCEF-Laverock is now offering a new counseling program that may interest you. Group counseling. Come . . . share . . . and grow through discipleship. Begin to take risks and relearn how to trust. (Ellipse in original.)
>
> Call today for more information. . . .[26]

A call to the number listed revealed that the group leader was Leslie Vernick. Even the idea of group counseling violates Adams' concerns addressed in "Group Therapy—or Slander" from *Essays on Counseling*.[27] The call also revealed that Vernick planned to use a 12-Step type of spiritual approach with this group.[28]

David Powlison

Besides being a staff member of CCEF, Powlison is a Lecturer in Practical Theology at Westminster Theological Seminary in Philadelphia and is the editor of *The Journal of Biblical Counseling* (formerly *The Journal of Pastoral Practice*). In one of Powlison's articles in *The Journal of Pastoral Practice*, he says:

> One of the ironies (whether it is bitter, humorous or sublime I am unsure!) attending the contemporary Christian counseling world is that **we, of all people, are the ones who successfully will "integrate" secular psychology**. "Integrationists" are too impressed with psychology's insights to be able to win them to Christ. Integrationists have missed the point that the big question between Christians and secular psychologists is not, "What can we learn from them?" The big question is, "How can we speak into their world to evangelize them?" But it is also fair to say that presuppositionalists have missed that the big question between biblical counseling and Christian integrationists is not, "How can we reject and avoid them?" The big question is, "How can we speak constructively into their world?" The key to both big questions is an ability to **reframe everything that psychologists see and hold dear into biblical categories**. If we do our homework, then biblical counseling not only will be a

message for the psychologized church. It will be a message for the psychologized world.[29] (Emphasis added.)

While others have integrated in a nonbiblical way, CCEF expects to "successfully . . . 'integrate' psychology" with "an ability to reframe everything that psychologists see and hold dear into biblical categories." That sounds like out and out integration.

Powlison goes on to say:

At minimum there are thousands of Christians, psychologists, psychiatrists, social workers, college psychology majors, counselees drinking from a different well who can be won by an approach that interacts with and radically reframes what enamors them about psychology.[30]

Just as Crabb thought that he could use just enough from secular psychology to fit into biblical categories and thereby form a biblical counseling that "interacts with and radically reframes what enamors them about psychology," Powlison reveals that he holds the same hope. But, what enamors people about psychology is that it appeals to the flesh. And just as Crabb denies being an integrationist, Powlison does not see that he is indeed advocating integration, a form of integration which he believes is superior to all others. But hasn't every Christian integrationist thought he was combining the best from both worlds through reframing (biblicizing) psychology to make it fit with Scripture?

In an article in the *Journal of Psychology and Theology*, Powlison says:

> . . . a biblical view of presuppositions provides a sharply distinct alternative to any and all forms of secularist thinking. It provides a truly coherent rationale for science. It provides a solid, biblical theoretical foundation for counseling people. It accounts for and **appreciates the insights of psychology** without losing sight of the pervasive distortion within each insight.[31] (Emphasis added.)

What insights? Every integrationist picks and chooses whatever "insights" he likes, and different integrationists will prefer different "insights." How is it that the Bible must be supplemented with such insights?

Powlison lists three questions at the conclusion of his article:

> 1. Does the momentum behind a particular idea come from Scripture or psychology?
> 2. Is the God-ward referent in immediate evidence when discussing human behavior, motives, norms, problems, solutions and so forth? Or is psychology the moving force in a system, and Scripture is employed essentially to window dress and prooftext?

3. Do the observations of psychology illustrate and apply biblical categories of thought about human life? Or is Scripture used to provide illustrations, applications and parallels to secular categories of thought?[32]

All the integrationists we know profess to believe that (1) Scripture comes first, (2) Scripture is the moving force in the system, (3) Scriptural categories of thought about human life are illustrated and applied through the observations of psychology. Powlison's article may help an integrationist clean up a little bit of his act, but it will surely affirm him as an integrationist and help him continue to use psychology in counseling.

Additionally, and more important, one can take any psychological system, no matter how ungodly or how satanic, and give it a "God-ward referent." Isn't that what Crabb has done so popularly by taking Freudian and, particularly, Adlerian ideas and fitting them into so-called biblical categories?[33] Crabb ended up with an ungodly psychological system that used God as the person who can make one worthwhile.[34] Powlison says, "Sin's character is to present itself as plausible truth."[35] Isn't that what the promoters of this type of psychology do?

Knowingly or not, Powlison has provided an academic, not biblical basis, for psychological integration. After reading Powlison, one can only conclude that he is an integrationist.

More Compromise

Powlison and Welch have both contributed to the book *Power Religion*. An overall statement describing the book says:

> The contributors to Power Religion would be quick to note that these disciplines [psychology] are not in themselves evil or unnecessary, but when they replace the unique evangelical message, they lose both biblical fidelity and public credibility.[36]

The statement regarding the specific "Power Within" section to which Powlison and Welch contributed is the following:

> The authors of this section do not intend to pronounce judgment on professional psychology as a discipline or practice, but on pop-psychology as a substitute for solid doctrinal and evangelical preaching, teaching, and pastoral leadership. Are pastors and others trading the job of producing answers to the ultimate questions for that of armchair psychologist?[37]

The two following quotations from Powlison's chapter are examples of his integrationist stance:

> Biblical thinking shows specific ways in which a checked and repentant psychology could be extremely useful. Valid psychology is neither a psychotherapy nor a speculative

pseudoscience competing with biblical truth. Valid psychology is an exploratory and illustrative science that must be submitted to biblical categories. Biblical thinking turns psychological interpretations and psychotherapeutic interventions inside out and upside down.[38]

Through this entire process of encountering psychology, the church is humbled and made wiser. To their credit, integrationists see that this must happen. The entire process affirms that secular psychologists are not stupid. It recognizes that the church is imperfect, ignorant, and loveless in certain pivotal ways.[39]

It is doubtful that Powlison's chapter offended any in the "Christian" psychology camp. We suspect that some of the Christian psychologists mentioned in the chapter, including Crabb, would not only say a hearty "Amen" to what Powlison has written, but recommend it to others. In fact, Crabb does recommend it to others.[40]

The May 17, 1993, issue of *Christianity Today* had an article by Tim Stafford titled "How Christian Psychology is Changing the Church." In the article he calls Dave Hunt, John MacArthur, and Martin and Deidre Bobgan "adamant critics." He describes another group as using "subtler criticisms" and says of them that **"they see some value in psychotherapy."**[41] Stafford includes David Powlison in this second group. Stafford also says, "David Powlison has developed a biblical understanding of counseling that accords with many of psychology's insights."[42]

One year later *Christianity Today* published an article titled "Psychobabble" by Dr. Robert C. Roberts. The subtitle is "A guide for perplexed Christians in an age of therapies." Roberts is professor of philosophy and psychological studies at Wheaton College and makes no pretense about his integrationist position. He says:

> Yet not only does each psychotherapy bear some resemblance to Christian psychology; each of them also, in one respect or another, contradicts Christianity. Our integration of insights and techniques from these other psychologies must therefore be done cautiously and with precision.[43]

In reference to the various therapies, Roberts refers positively to "their insights" and their "special techniques for person formation." He says that "it stands to reason that we can learn a lot through dialogue with them." Roberts says, "Christian psychotherapy will be 'eclectic' in bearing a number of resemblances to the secular therapies; some of these will be the result of its integrating features of those other therapies."[44]

The article and what Roberts says did not surprise us. Nor were we surprised to see an interview with David Powlison inserted on a page midway through Roberts' integrationist article.[45] Considering Stafford's above comment about Powlison, it also made sense that he was the one to interview him for the issue featuring Roberts' article. If Powlison disagreed with Stafford's characterization of him in his article "How Christian Psychology is Changing the Church," it certainly did not come out in this interview published one year later.

In the earlier issue of *Christianity Today*, there is a section on "How to Choose a Counselor." The article is a strong endorsement for professional, trained, licensed counselors. There is a definite message that professional counselors are better able than pastors, elders, and other lay people to counsel individuals. In seeking a counselor, one is supposed to ask about the counselor's graduate degree "from an accredited (not just state-approved), reputable university or seminary." The article suggests seeking licensed individuals "in places where licensing laws exist."[46] It also suggests that the individual be certified "by a nationally recognized association." The article categorically states: "Steer clear of counselors who do not have at least a master's degree in counseling or in a related field of study from an accredited university or seminary." It also says, "Reject those unlicensed by the state or province, if there are licensing laws, or not certified by a reputable, nationally known association of psychologists, counselors, or pastors. Degrees and licenses should be framed and displayed where clients can see and read them easily."[47]

The same issue of *Christianity Today* included a paid directory listing for the American Association of Christian Counselors (AACC) and the Christian Association for Psychological Studies (CAPS). These two organizations believe in integrating psychology and the Bible. In the directory there are listings of professionals from all over America, as well as listings for treatment centers and training programs. There is one listing that did not surprise us. It is the one for CCEF.[48] Now, if the paid listing of CCEF had been separated from the article on how to choose a counselor and separated from the group of integrationist therapists and organizations, we may have had no problem with it. But, if CCEF had been concerned about being listed among integrationists, they could have asked who else would be advertising with them in that special section. The issue of *Christianity Today* that featured Roberts' article "Psychobabble" also carried a section called "Christian Counseling Directory."[49] It was the same melange of offerings that occurred a year earlier. CCEF once again placed its listing along with the other integrationists.[50]

Conclusion

In conclusion, we believe those at CCEF have compromised the clear message of Scripture and have devalued their birthright with psychological pottage. But CCEF is only one example of many who have drifted into integration. There are many other counseling ministries that seemed to start out well, but then moved their focus from Christ's pasture to the grass on the psychological side of the fence. The pull of the world is consistently powerful. As soon as any of us adds the world's ways to the Lord's ways, we weaken, rather than strengthen, the ministry of personal care in the body of Christ. What was meant to be a solution to the influx of psychology into Christianity has, for many, drifted into a compromise with it. What was meant to be a return to biblically-based pastoral care and mutual ministry slid back into a reflection of the very problem it was meant to solve.

We need more, not less, separation from secular psychology and all those who have attempted to integrate it. For all the reasons given in this book, we urge all biblical counselors and all biblical counseling ministries to abandon all practices that reflect the world and to return to biblically-based pastoral and mutual care. We are opposed to the present condition and operation of those biblical counseling ministries that have slipped, particularly those that have slid right out of the biblically ordained ministries of the church. Yes, we are against biblical counseling, but **we are for the Bible**. We continue to encourage Christians to minister to one another through the Word of God, the guidance and enabling of the Holy Spirit, and the Bible-based ministries of the church.

6

Recycling or Integration?

Why would anyone want to integrate psychology and Scripture under any circumstances? The sad truth is that many who call themselves biblical counselors either directly and proudly integrate or are integrationists in disguise. As we have shown in the previous chapter, one of many such groups and individuals is the Christian Counseling and Educational Foundation (CCEF).

We quote from the CCEF Catalog a course description as follows:

This course considers how Christian counseling relates to secular psychotherapies. The

course **avoids their wholesale acceptance** ("integration") which destroys Scripture's authority. It also **avoids outright
rejection, which robs the Christian
counselor of the stimulus of secular
insights**. Instead, a **"recycling"** model is
proposed to maintain the Bible sufficiency as
well as sharpen your understanding of biblical teaching. **This recycling model is then
applied to various schools of counseling, e.g., Freudian, Skinnerian, Rogerian, Adlerian, cognitive, behavioral and
family systems**. The result is familiarity
with existing psychotherapies, greater skill
in using Scripture apologetically and a growing **arsenal of methods to use to
enhance biblical change.**[1] (Emphasis
added.)

Please note that "wholesale acceptance" of "secular
psychotherapies" is called "integration" at CCEF.
They admit they avoid "outright rejection [of secular psychotherapies], which robs the Christian
counselor of the stimulus of secular insights."

CCEF avoids both "wholesale acceptance" and
"outright rejection" of "secular psychotherapies."
What is their position? It is a "recycling model." We
repeat what they say:

Instead, a **"recycling"** model is proposed to
maintain the Bible sufficiency as well as
sharpen your understanding of biblical
teaching. **This recycling model is then**

applied to various schools of counseling, e.g., Freudian, Skinnerian, Rogerian, Adlerian, cognitive, behavioral and family systems. The result is familiarity with existing psychotherapies, greater skill in using Scripture apologetically and a growing **arsenal of methods to use to enhance biblical change**. (Emphasis added.)[2]

That sounds like an integration position. *Recycling* is merely a euphemism for *integrating*. The only apparent difference in the minds of those at CCEF is that integrationists are involved in "wholesale acceptance" of "secular psychotherapies" and that CCEF is not. Instead, CCEF claims to be involved in recycling. What is recycling? The above quote from the CCEF catalog reveals that they recycle "secular psychotherapies." Since CCEF is not into "wholesale acceptance" of "secular psychotherapies," the implication is that their "recycling model" is perfectly acceptable. But, no integrationist among the many we have critiqued would admit to "wholesale acceptance" of "secular psychotherapies." By CCEF's definition of *recycling*, all of the integrationists we know could describe themselves as "recyclers."

What is this recycling CCEF is doing? As an example of CCEF recycling, we will critique a series of talks given by Dr. John Bettler, Director of CCEF. The following analysis of Bettler's use of Adlerian psychology, regardless of the definitions used for *recycling* and *integration*, will reveal that what CCEF does with "recycling" cannot be acceptable as biblical counseling.

As mentioned earlier, Bettler is a member of the North American Society of Adlerian Psychology (NASAP), referred to as "the home of Adlerians." One goal of NASAP is "fulfilling human potential." Another NASAP goal is "to promote the growth and understanding of Adlerian psychology." Regarding our concern about Bettler's membership in NASAP, David Powlison says:

> Having heard him [Bettler] talk about it, it is interesting to know what he thinks about NASAP. . . . It proves him to be an opponent of integrationistic thinking. . . . You've never heard the blistering critique Bettler makes of Adler, so it's of course legitimate to raise the question as to whether membership constitutes endorsement.[3]

In the following critique, we will demonstrate that, call it what you may, Bettler is integrating (recycling) Adlerian psychology. The end result is not biblical. Keep in mind that Bettler has been and remains a member of NASAP, thoroughly knows Adlerian psychology, has taught Adlerian psychology, and knows the principles and terminology of Adlerian psychology. Those Adlerian principles and terminology are transparent in his presentation.

Recycling Adler

Bettler believes in and promotes recycling. What follows is an excellent example of CCEF recycling. It is the recycling of Adlerian psychology in biblical terms. But, the Bible must be twisted by Bettler to support his Adlerian beliefs! If there is any question that what Bettler is teaching is Adlerian psychology, ask anyone who knows Adlerian psychology to read "Towards a 'Confession of Faith' in the Past" in *The Biblical Counselor*[4] and "Counseling and the Problem of the Past" in *The Journal of Biblical Counseling*,[5] or listen to Bettler's three taped messages from the CCEF June Institute (1993).

At the CCEF 1993 Summer Institute, Bettler presented a series of three messages titled "Dealing with a Person's Past."[6] Bettler's arguments for exploring the past and his proposed use of the past in counseling not only reveal his Adlerian background, but show his commitment to recycling Adler, without even referring to Adler or crediting him in any way. This glaring omission enables those listeners who are not acquainted with Adlerian Individual Psychology to suppose that Bettler's proposed use of the past comes solely from Scripture.

Alfred Adler (1870-1937) began as an associate of Freud, but broke away from him as he developed his own theory of Individual Psychology. While his theory contained many of Freud's ideas, such as a modified psychic determinism, unconscious motivation, and the importance of a patient gaining insight into his unconscious motives and assumptions, he did not believe people were motivated by sexual impulses.[7] Instead, he believed that "striving for superiority" was the universal motivation of mankind. Adler believed that humans are motivated by a need to overcome feelings of inferiority and to become superior. He further taught that everyone has the same goal of superiority but that early in life (around age five) each person develops his own **"style of life"** for pursuing his goal.[8]

Adler also theorized a doctrine of the **"creative self,"** which proposes that man creates his own personality, gives meaning to life, and creates his own goals and means of reaching them.[9] Adler's humanistic theory of personality imputed to man righteousness, humanitarianism, uniqueness, dignity, worth, and power to direct and change one's own life.[10] Ironically Adler believed that the constant striving for superiority is what motivates mankind to be socially responsive and personally responsible.

Three Talks on the Past

In his first of three talks, Bettler opens the door to a variety of approaches in so-called biblical counseling and sets some reasonably sounding parameters for using the past, which, incidentally, are compatible with his Adlerian approach. In his second talk Bettler gives biblical justification for remembering and talking about the past, but he ends up forcing Scripture to **imply what it does not say** concerning the use of the past in counseling. In his final talk Bettler speaks about how using the past reveals a person's "manner of life" and therefore gives a key to understanding what really needs to be changed in addition to present thinking and behaving. In this final talk Bettler is presenting an only slightly altered Adlerian approach, including Adler's theories of "style of life" and the "creative self."

Setting the Stage

Before getting into the subject of the past, Bettler sets the stage by talking about how there are differences in approach among those who call themselves "biblical counselors." He begins his first talk with a story about football to illustrate the following point: "Some of us who call ourselves biblical counselors play the game differently." He then expands on this idea by saying that some counselors emphasize what a person does over what he is feeling. Some take time to understand how a person thinks. Some are concerned with motivation and others are not. Because biblical counselors may counsel differently from one another, CCEF wants to come up with parameters for what one must adhere to in order to be called a biblical counselor.

Bettler says that although Christians have different beliefs with respect to baptism and eschatology, for instance, it is their agreement on the fundamentals of the faith that counts. Likewise, he notes that biblical counselors may counsel differently, but still agree on the fundamentals of the faith. This is possibly a false analogy, depending on what might be included in "biblical counseling." The same analogy is often cited by integrationists, and, when it is, it is a false analogy, because such theological differences within orthodox fundamentals of the faith are differences of interpretation of Scripture, not differences arising from the inclusion of secular material!

At this point in his first talk, Bettler declares what a dangerous job it is to draw lines about what is and what is not biblical counseling. He even goes so far as to say that if you narrow the circle too closely "you're pushing towards the cults." However, we are concerned! In delineating what is biblical counseling, will CCEF truly stick with Scripture? Or, will they continue to recycle secular theories, integrate them into biblical counseling, and then say that such inclusion is just the same as peripheral theological differences? That is our concern!

Bettler further sets the stage for his beliefs about the importance of the past in counseling by presenting several counseling cases. The first case is a woman whose "husband is a driven type." In counseling she says that her brother had sexually abused her when she was a child. Furthermore, her description of her brother is exactly like that of her husband. Then Bettler asks, "Is there a connection?" The second case is about a wife who keeps bringing up her husband's adultery after he has confessed and repented. Bettler asks, "Is there something about this experience that rings other bells?" He wonders if there are "things in the past not yet dealt with." The questions Bettler asks in reference to these cases reveal something about his theoretical orientation, which will become evident as he moves along. **He is looking for clues in the person's past to tell him something special about the person, and that is an important aspect of Adlerian psychology.**

Bettler does speak a word of caution about memory and the current fad of people seeing themselves as victims and looking to their past to explain and deal with their present. Yet, even this caution fits with an Adlerian perspective, because Adler did not believe that people are victims of their past. He taught that people creatively interact with their circumstances and are thereby responsible. In concert with Adler, Bettler criticizes people looking to their past simply to explain and thereby deal with their present. However, as he reveals later in his talk, Bettler teaches the Adlerian theory about exploring a person's past to find clues for discovering one's "manner of life" or "style of life."

Biblical Support?

In his second talk Bettler attempts to support his use of the past in counseling by citing instances in Scripture where God instructed His people to remember certain events in their history. Bettler declares, "The past is important because God asks us to remember certain things." He then speaks of how "memories can be very rewarding" and how wonderful it is to remember the godly men who were influential in his life. He says, "Paul tells us to remember those who labor among us," and concludes that "memory is a good thing." Bettler follows an illogical progression when he says, "The past is important because God asks us to remember certain things" and when he states a generality that "memory is a good thing." Just because "God asks us to remember **certain** things," does it follow that "the past is important"? What about the past is important? Everything? No, but Bettler is preparing his audience to accept his later conclusion: that exploring the past in counseling is important if a counselor is to know how to counsel that person.

Bettler next presents three things God tells us to remember: (1) the Passover and exodus from Egypt, (2) the Lord's Supper, and (3) the sins of Israel. After giving some details about the importance of remembering God's miraculous deliverance of the Israelites out of Egypt, Bettler declares: "God doesn't want us to forget." Thus, he takes an extremely significant incident from the history of God's dealings with Israel and makes a generalized statement, "God doesn't want us to forget." While this statement is imbedded in the history of Israel, we find that Bettler is working towards the importance of one's **personal** past in counseling. Thus, his generalized statement will have broad meanings as he goes along. Just because we are to remember specifics A, B & C (the **national** past of Israel), it does not necessarily follow that we are to remember, focus on and find present help from remembering D, E & F (the **personal** past of one's life).

Bettler's second point has to do with remembering the Lord's Supper, the memorial instituted by Jesus Himself to help believers remember the salvation He purchased for them and to look forward to His return. However, this memory is focused on the Lord, not on self or on incidents from one's childhood. This very memorial is a reminder that we are new creatures in Christ and that we are to live by His life, not by searching our personal past for clues for improving our present. Paul's passion, expressed in Philippians 3, matches this memorial better than any counseling modality that searches a prechristian past for help in present living. Paul only mentions his own personal past to say that, no matter how glorious it might have seemed at the time, it was the dung of striving for righteousness through the law. Therefore, he declares, "But this one thing I do, forgetting those things which are behind, and reaching forth unto those things which are before, I press toward the mark for the prize of the high calling of God in Christ Jesus" (Philippians 3:13,14).

National Past versus Personal Past

Bettler's third piece of evidence about the importance of the past is that of Paul reminding his readers about the sins of the Israelites so that they would not repeat the same sins. However, Paul is not referring to personal past sins, but rather to the historical past sins of a nation that sinned against God. He is saying that these "are written for our admonition" so that we will not repeat them. However, Bettler seems to apply these verses as though they are referring to one's own personal past when he says, "The past is there so that I won't get conceited in the present and that I'll be encouraged to handle whatever difficulty, whatever trial comes to me in the present." Is it really the past that does this? Or is it the reality of Christ in the believer?

Throughout this entire section of his talk, Bettler uses examples of the historic past regarding what God did for the nation of Israel, what Christ accomplished on the cross, and the sins of Israel in light of God's goodness to them. The first two examples are about the history of God and His work and the third is about the history of a nation in rebellion against the very God of salvation. These are examples of the national historic past (not one's personal past) to reveal the goodness of God and the sinfulness of man, whereby we might know Him better and be warned against following the ways of the flesh. These examples are about the history of God in relation to His people rather than the history of one's own personal past. Bettler makes no distinction, however, because he wants these examples to serve his purpose: to show that the personal past is important in counseling.

After presenting the three examples, which do not at all prove the importance of the personal past in counseling, Bettler draws three conclusions: (1) that God explains the past, (2) that "past events push into the present," and (3) that the "past reaches into the future." Yes, God does explain his dealings with men to give them understanding concerning His purposes and what their responses should be. Bettler says that God acts in history and then explains his actions. But, just because God is the interpreter of His dealings with Israel, does it follow that a counselor is to interpret a "counselee's" past? Certainly Scripture does give an explanation concerning our past. We were born in sin, fulfilled the lusts of the flesh and the desires of the mind, and were "by nature the children of wrath." However, as Bettler later reveals, that explanation is apparently not detailed enough for his type of biblical counseling, because he suggests using the past in ways that are beyond Scripture and into the realm of speculation, similar to Adler's use of the past.

Bettler's second point, that "past events push into the present," seems obvious in that we do live in a space/time dimension, and we may presently suffer the consequences of past sins and presently benefit from God's blessings poured out in the past. But, will Bettler use this simple statement for a more complex purpose for utilizing the past in counseling? He says, "Memories are for present living." Again, he uses such a broad generalization that one wonders what he means. What memories? How far back is Bettler talking about? Infancy? Early childhood? Yesterday? Naturally we have to remember how to drive a car in order to drive one today and we have to remember what we have learned and what the Bible says. However, Bettler is using this idea, "Memories are for present living," to support a particular use of past personal memories in counseling.

Bettler's third point, that "the past reaches into the future," is another highly generalized statement to which he adds, "The past is God's context for the person in the present." How so? The past of what He has accomplished and provided? No. Bettler uses this to support using the personal past, which is now to be examined in counseling so that the counselor can better understand the "counselee" and so that the "counselee" can overcome his problems of living. Evidently every aspect of a person's past is important to Bettler because he declares, "God wrote your story."

An Old Testament "Eddie Haskell"?

To illustrate the importance of each person's past, Bettler gives a highly speculative interpretation of Joseph's past. If this is the kind of interpretation he gives to anyone's past, one has to expect a great deal of speculation. Bettler describes Joseph as a brat and says, "Joseph was probably the Eddie Haskell of the Old Testament." While it is true that when Joseph was seventeen years old he "brought unto his father [his brothers'] evil report," to compare Joseph with a bratty television character whose stock character role was one of getting other kids into trouble and then acting like an innocent angel by "kissing up" to the adults is incredible. **Bettler's interpretation of Joseph's childhood (which is not even recorded in Scripture) is his own Adlerian fabrication made up of unfounded assumptions, suppositions, and conjectures.** This is an unfortunate interpretation for two reasons: there is no scriptural basis for such an interpretation and the interpretation does not in any way match the kind of person Joseph was throughout the hardships imposed upon him in Egypt. There is no evidence of brattiness, no confession of brattiness, and no pattern of brattiness.

Bettler then says, "When I counsel someone, I want to know his story. I want to know how his present problems fit into his narrative, how his present problem, whatever it is, is a unique part of what God has done and is doing in his life." But, when Bettler hears a person's story (as he reads the story of Joseph in the Bible) will he then give his own interpretation based upon a television character? Bettler continues:

> So the past is important because God asks us to remember certain things. The past helps us to understand God's context for that person. It helps us to understand his story.

Adler's "Creative Self" Recycled

Bettler continues this assumption that, just because God asks us to "remember certain things" having to do with His goodness and Israel's sinfulness, anyone's personal past "is important," and that past "helps us to understand God's context for the person." Building upon this faulty foundation, Bettler presses on. And, here is where some of his Adlerian roots begin to surface. Bettler says, "The past influences the counselee," and, "The counselee influences the past." Regarding the stresses that occur in our lives, Bettler declares that "we influence those stresses as much as those stresses influence us." He says, "We are creatively responding to those things that happen to us."

Especially noteworthy is Bettler's use of the words *creatively responding*. The concept of the "creative self" is considered to be "Adler's crowning achievement as a personality theorist." Adler's theory of the creative self is that each person creates his own personality through a combination of "stimuli acting upon the person and the responses he makes to these stimuli."[11] Or, as Bettler expresses it, "We influence those stresses as much as those stresses influence us," and, "We are creatively responding to those things that happen to us." Is this similarity an accident? Did Bettler discover that idea in Scripture? Or had Adler presented a new "truth" to mankind to enable Christian counselors to understand why people are the way they are?

Bettler says, "We creatively interpret the things that have happened to us." Adler says in reference to man making his own personality out of heredity and environment:

> Heredity only endows him with certain abilities. Environment only gives him certain impressions. These abilities and impressions, and the manner in which he "experiences" them—that is to say, the interpretation he makes of these experiences— are the bricks which he uses in his own "creative" way in building up his attitude toward life. It is his individual way of using these bricks, or in other words his attitude toward life, which determines this relationship to the outside world.[12]

Bettler's statement is simply a shortened paraphrase of Adler. He is saying the same thing as Adler, only without mentioning his source. This is an example of how "recycling" works: Christians take notions from secular psychologists, put them into some type of biblical framework (i.e., God telling the "Israelites to remember certain things"), and then teach them as biblical principles of counseling without even giving proper credit to the original theorist. One thing is clear, however. Once a Christian begins to see things through the theories of secularists, he will begin to see Scripture according to those notions. He will think he is counseling biblically, when he is simply being an integrationist. In this case, "recycling" is no different from what Larry Crabb and others believe they have done.[13]

Adler's ideas about the "creative self" grew out of his theory of "style of life," which is called "the most distinctive feature of his psychology." These two notions are so closely interwoven that it is difficult to separate them. According to Adler, each person develops his own unique way of reaching his goals during the first four or five years of life. Once the person's style of life is formed, his own unique style (including attitudes and feelings) remains relatively fixed throughout his entire lifetime. Through his own unique style of life, a person's creative self interacts with its environment and interprets reality in such a way as to create and reach its own characteristic goal.[14]

Adler's theories are ways of interpreting what people do. They are at the same level of scientific validity as the collected, often contradictory notions of the now over 450 different psychological counseling approaches. It is possible to use any of these theoretical frameworks to view humanity, but these are merely the lenses of human interpretation, mainly based upon the personal experiences of the various theorists themselves. What Adler and others contributed is not simply objective observations about what people do. Instead, they sought through their own fallenness to see into the inner man.

We have no problem with Bettler referring to objective observations made by research psychologists who follow the strict procedures of scientific research and give information about aspects of memory. However, there are huge differences between description and interpretation, and between description and prescription. Thus, some of Bettler's remarks about memory do not intrude upon Scripture, which is the only basis for understanding why man is the way he is, why he does what he does, and how he is to change. Bettler's three words about memory, that it is *active, selective*, and *creative*, are descriptive rather than speculative. However, when he attempts to delve into the why's and wherefore's of the creative aspect of memory and turns it into a person "creatively reinterpret[ing] his own history," Bettler moves from simple description to speculative interpretation and prescriptive treatment methods.

Bettler says:

When I talk to a counselee about his past, the last thing I'm interested in is what happened. Now that may sound strange, but there's no way I'm ever going to know what happened. What I'm going to find out is what he remembers happened, and that will tell me an awful lot about what he thinks and believes and values today.

What Bettler is looking for is not history, but a life style. He is looking for exactly what Adler looked for with his method of early childhood recollections, which served as clues to a "counselee's" style of life, his own unique manner of life, lifetime goal, and means of reaching that goal.

Bettler has an interesting way of using observations found by memory researchers to build a bridge to his recycled form of Adler's creative self and style of life. Bettler says:

These scientists are finding that in the formation of a memory—get this—current beliefs about past events are more important than what actually happened. This is why an event that seemed trivial when we were children can be reinterpreted and given new emotional significance when we are adults and visa versa.

Bettler's reference to current memory research does only one thing for his recycled Adlerian model and methodology. It tells us that any person's story is limited to incomplete memory, filled in with details that seem to make sense at the time. However, Bettler seems to think that a recreated memory will give clues to the counselor about how the "counselee" has misshaped his memories, since he declares: "We can misshape memories to fit the lies that we believe now about ourselves, about others, about God."

It apparently does not matter to Bettler if the memory of a "counselee" is accurate or not—only how it affects that person now. He says, "The past is simply a way to get into the present to help me and to help the counselee understand his story." Thus it does not appear to matter to Bettler if a person was truly abused or not. After all, the purpose of the past is only to understand a person's story in order to discover his "manner of life" or life style. Bettler says:

> These conclusions are being lived out in the present and what we have to do then is look at the false ways (that is the ungodly or the unbiblical ways) this person has processed that event and get the person to look at it God's way.

While this may sound biblical on the surface, what Bettler is asking for is an unbiblical exploration into the "old man," to find help for present obedience. He is asking us to look into the past to find the "false ways." (Why doesn't he call them "sinful ways"?) Evidently he believes we have to examine our personal past in detail in order to know what to put off (Ephesians 4:22). While this might be great counseling for the flesh to improve itself, Bettler has not yet demonstrated the importance of examining a person's past in order to walk according to the Spirit in obedience to the Lord.

Using the Past in Counseling

So far during these talks, Bettler has been laying the groundwork for presenting his methods of using the past in counseling. He begins his third message by making a number of assertions. He says:

> You process the things I say according to all of the things you've been experiencing recently and maybe for a long period of time.

> There is no fact without interpretation. There's no event without a process of creatively interacting with that.

> Everybody interprets it according to his own mindset, his own values.

> Who knows whether you're getting it [what he is saying to his audience] or not because you're creatively interpreting it.

We're sure Adlerians would agree with Bettler's assertions. **Alfred Adler couldn't have said it any better!**

Now Bettler describes one of the many secular views of the past, but he calls it "the secular view."

He states that the "secular view says this child is not only a victim of these things. He is powerless when these things come upon him. He is also a closed system." Bettler rightly denigrates the notions of catharsis and the hydraulic model of man. However, when he contrasts this "secular view" he makes it sound as though his contrasting view is not secular, when, in fact, it is recycled Adler. Bettler contrasts the "secular" model with the idea that whatever comes into a child's life, such as stresses and good things, are also being acted upon by the child. He says, "These things are coming to bear on the child, but the child is influencing them." Bettler continues:

> He [the child] isn't passive. He is an active processor. He isn't a victim only; he is an interpreter. He looks at all these things that happen to him and he makes some very basic conclusions about others, about God, about himself, about what's important, about what's not important. He doesn't just lie there like a lump of clay that is shaped and pushed by all of these things. This child is an image bearer of God. And what that means is he acts aggressively with what happens to him. God is an interpreter. God interacts creatively with his creation and so does the child who is created in the image of God.

Until Bettler reaches the part about being created in the image of God, he is perfectly

describing Adler's creative self who is not left to be a victim of circumstances. Then, when he attempts to justify his description by making this the interpretation of what it means to be created in the image of God, Bettler again slips into speculation.

Adler's "Style of Life" Recycled

At this point Bettler introduces what he calls the "biblical view." He declares that a "counselee" has other resources besides bad events that may have occurred in his life. He says:

> I also have his creative interpretation. And what those things form is what I'm going to call a manner of life. And this manner of life shows itself in the present.

Adlerians would have to admit that **Bettler's "manner of life" is none other than Adler's "style of life"!**

Bettler continues:

> The life he's living now is the sum total of all the conclusions he has made about what makes life work. And if he has made those conclusions, then those conclusions are a lie because they are not what God says make things work. Then there's hope because he can change those conclusions. He can start thinking about what has happened in his life the way God says he ought to think about what happens in his life.

The part about "all the conclusions he has made about what makes life work" is definitely Adlerian because Adler's style of life is made up of all that helps a person reach his goal of making his life work. The recycling or integration comes when he brings in what "God says make things work," thus making God the way to make things work.

Adler is particularly appealing because some of what he says does seem true, at least at the descriptive level. However, one has to be extremely careful, because if we take from Adler what sounds biblical or what does not seem to be antibiblical, we can very easily be enticed to draw more from Adler than Scripture would permit. That is exactly what is wrong with recycling. Adler seems to make so much sense in some respects (as do other psychological theorists) that it is easy to start viewing Scripture from a viewpoint influenced by his teachings. Besides the possibility of contamination, there is the profound risk of strengthening the flesh while rendering the counseling powerless as far as the spiritual man is concerned.

Along with every secular theory of why people are the way they are, why they do what they do, and how they change is a methodology. Adler taught that talking about early childhood events could reveal a person's style of life and that if a person could understand his style and how it was not working he could change. He could replace false beliefs with true beliefs. He could replace ways that did not work towards his goal with ways that might work. He could even see that perhaps his goal was the wrong goal.

Bettler says, "The past is a way of revealing the counselee's manner of life, and that phrase comes from Ephesians 4:17 and following." Ephesians 4:17-24:

> This I say therefore, and testify in the Lord, that ye henceforth walk not as other Gentiles walk, in the vanity of their mind, Having the understanding darkened, being alienated from the life of God through the ignorance that is in them, because of the blindness of their heart: Who being past feeling have given themselves over unto lasciviousness, to work all uncleanness with greediness. But ye have not so learned Christ; If so be that ye have heard him, and have been taught by him, as the truth is in Jesus: That ye put off concerning the **former conversation** [*anastrophe*] the old man, which is corrupt according to the deceitful lusts; And be renewed in the spirit of your mind; And that ye put on the new man, which after God is created in righteousness and true holiness.

Bettler's model and methodology come from Adler. The convenient modern translation of *anastrophe* into *manner of life* gives him a way to recycle Adler's style of life into his supposedly biblical model and methodology.

Bettler mentions how Jay Adams made Ephesians 4:22-24 famous in reference to putting off and putting on. Then he says, "But let's look at it from a slightly different perspective." He then reads the verse from the NASB (New American Standard Bible) and says that the word *anastrophe* (but he must be referring to the verb form, *anastrepho*) could even be translated "to return . . . to turn again." With this possibility Bettler says:

> So when Paul talked here about this former manner of life he's talking about that to which you turn to again and again and again and again. . . the values that you turn to again and again and again . . .the beliefs . . . the habits . . . the behavior patterns you turn to again and again and again.

Bettler says Adams calls these "habit patterns" or "behavioral patterns." Bettler continues:

> But it's more than just habits. It's more than just the behaviors that are observed. Look at verse 17 . . . Paul says it's a walk. . . . It refers to the person, the whole manner of life.

What Bettler is calling for is finding out about a person's internal style of life. He is trying to use the past to understand the person's style of life so that he can know the thoughts and intentions of the heart. But, that is the work of the Word of God and the Spirit of God. Looking into the soul of another person to discover his manner of life and thereby to help him change is assuming the role of God Himself. If human counselors do that, they will slip into speculation. They will misinterpret the past just as surely as Bettler did with his Joseph-equals-Eddie-Haskell interpretation through speculating on Joseph's manner of life.

Bettler declares that everything about a person is summed up in his manner of life. Indeed, that is a good, though shallow, description of Adler's "style of life." Bettler continues:

> My point in a nutshell: **If you're going to do counseling, you've got to know the person's manner of life**, and when you talk about the past and the counselee talks about his past, your purpose is not to uncover history; your purpose is to uncover his *anastrophe*, his **manner of life**, the way he has processed all of those things that have happened to him and brought them into a **style of life**. (Emphasis added.)

Notice the great importance Bettler puts on the past and getting to know the person's manner of life, "the way he has processed all of those things that have happened to him and brought them into a style of life." That is internal. Bettler's use of the term *manner of life* refers to the inner man, the way he internally interprets his life and tries to make it work. Also, notice that **Bettler even uses Adler's terminology here—style of life**.

In Adlerian psychology, the first phase of therapy consists of the therapist establishing rapport with the patient. The second phase is devoted to learning "to understand the patient's life style and goal."[15] This consists of gaining insight into the patient's motivations, his inner intentions. Adlerian therapy is generally long-term. After extensive analysis to determine the life style, the therapist has to convince the client of his findings and then help him change through small increments of insight over the months and even years of therapy. Adlerian case histories include such phrases as "A year went by," "almost two years into therapy," and "during the two and a half years of treatment."[16]

For an Adlerian, understanding a patient's life style is very important. Bettler shows how important this is to him when he declares: "If you're going to do counseling, you've got to know the person's manner of life . . . the way he has processed all of those things that have happened to him and brought them into a style of life."

Bettler lists the many things about the "counselee" that the counselor must search for in the "counselee's" past. Most of them are subjective and internal and have to do with the nonphysical aspect of man. The notion Bettler seems to be presenting is that the past is the counselor's key to knowing a person's heart, his inner man. But, of course, one must know how to turn that key, how to elicit portions of the past and mix in the elixir of interpretation.

However, Bettler is not simply presenting Adlerian Individual Psychology. He is presenting his own recycled version and thus integrates the idea of repentance. The counselor uses the past to unlock the present so that the "counselee" can repent from "the wrong conclusions and styles he's developed over the years" in addition to present sins. It is understandable that Adler would attempt to work on the inner person, the soul, the creative self, because he did not believe that the Word of God and the Holy Spirit do that inner work. Unfortunately, in recycling Adler, Bettler is attempting to go beyond what human counselors can really do. He is attempting to use the past as a key to understanding the present manner of life so that he can know the inner man and, with this secret knowledge, help the "counselee" understand himself and thereby change. Human counselors for too long have attempted to do the work only God can do.

Reinterpreting Scripture

Bettler desires to be biblical, but it appears that he also desires what he has gleaned from Adler to be biblical as well. He turns again to Scripture to prop up his recycled Adlerian theory. He turns to Genesis 32 and the story of Jacob. Bettler says:

> The person actively interprets, creatively interprets the things that happen to him and on the basis of those conclusions develops a manner of life, a characteristic **style of life**, *anastrophe*. (Emphasis added.)

Bettler has an imaginary counselor asking Jacob why he's afraid after he hears the news of Esau coming to meet him. He then refers to Jacob's manner of life beginning when he "came forth holding on to Esau's heel." His manner of life was "supplanter." Bettler then asks his audience to use their imagination (which is necessary in Adlerian counseling), proceeds to fictionalize the story of Jacob, and speculates that Jacob's inner voice kept saying, "Jacob, get a hold of life and don't let go" (very Adlerian). Bettler further speculates that Jacob's mother was "probably filling his mind with this thing about being contentious, being aggressive, getting a hold of his brother and not letting go and that means you gotta get ahead." This is a very Adlerian interpretation of Jacob, with his goal to "get ahead" and his style of hanging on and "not letting go," which was gleaned from an early childhood event, in this case Jacob's birth.

Bettler's words regarding Jacob, "and that means you gotta get ahead," reveal Jacob's goal according to Bettler's interpretation. Identifying the goal and the means by which a particular individual is attempting to reach that goal (such as, "getting a hold" and "not letting go") and then trying to help that person discover better goals and means to the goals are characteristic of Adlerian psychology. In his book *The Pattern of Life*, Adler wrote:

> The "cure" of the neurosis depends on the art of giving the neurotic insight into his errors and the demonstration of the inefficiency of his technique together with the encouragement to find better goals and patterns.[17]

Thus Bettler has an imaginary counselor explore Jacob's past to gain insight into his style (manner) of life.

After Bettler presents this great insight about Jacob's manner of life ("you gotta get ahead"), through an imaginary counselor with an imaginative interpretation of Scripture, he says Jacob needs an encounter with God. Bettler rightly declares that "Jacob needed a much more radical change than just learning how to deal with Esau." But then he adds, "He needed his manner of life changed." Yes, Jacob did need a more radical change, but it's the kind God does. We play God when we try to do it according to the fleshly means of recycled Adlerian style of life theories. Nevertheless, Bettler is so committed to style of life theories that he declares that it's "pretty dangerous to give assignments if you don't understand the *anastrophe*, manner of life."

That means a biblical counselor had better not assign any Bible reading or change of behavior until he discovers the "counselee's" style of life— and that might take quite a long time unless the counselor is adept at quickly jumping to conclusions. The implications of it being "pretty dangerous to give assignments if you don't understand the *anastrophe*, manner of life" should stop any preacher in his tracks. This makes dangerous all sermons that direct behavior change, such as telling people to love their neighbors and forgive one another for Christ's sake. That could even imply that reading the Bible is dangerous.

Why didn't Bettler describe Jacob's manner of life as wanting God's blessings, or believing God's promises and thinking he had to help God fulfill those promises? Was Rebecca merely wanting her son to get ahead or was she trying to help God fulfill His promises to her—that the older would serve the younger. The "gotta get ahead" life style identification of Jacob distorts Scripture and totally leaves out Jacob and Rebecca's attempts to help God fulfill His promises. Incidentally, attempting to understand any historical person from the Bible with any psychological theory, such as Bettler's Adlerian interpretation of Jacob, or a Jungian's use of archetypes (i.e., the trickster) or the popular use of the four temperaments, perverts Scripture to support a pet theory.

People are often confused about what is biblical. One easy way to make a psychological model **appear** biblical is to use it to interpret Scripture or to analyze a biblical character. That can be very deceptive. Using a psychological model to interpret Scripture does not make the model itself biblical. Instead, it distorts the very Word of God.

Bettler's interpretation of Jacob is an example of what Bettler will look for when he searches a person's past. If a counselor follows Bettler's example, he will look for the "counselee's" style of life and come up with a simplistic, one dimensional trait by which to describe and explain the person. He will probably find no more depth in such wild speculation as he would if he were to use the four temperaments, astrology, or personality testing. He may easily end up with a stock character, see everything about him through a slogan-type description, and help him make some changes for better or worse. Can anyone's life be summed up by such a slogan as "You gotta do anything you gotta do to get ahead"? That isn't any more specific, really, than what the Bible already tells us about ourselves.

A Biblical View of Manner of Life

How would you like to spill out your heart to a counselor and have him identify your "manner of life" as "You gotta do anything you gotta do to get ahead"? Would you truly know more about yourself than before? Would such information help you change? Why not simply recognize the truth of Scripture when it describes the former *anastrophe* of all of us?

> And you hath he quickened, who were dead in trespasses and sins: Wherein in time past ye walked according to the course of this world, according to the prince of the power of the air, the spirit that now worketh in the children of disobedience: Among whom also we all had our conversation in times past in the lusts of our flesh, fulfilling the desires of the flesh and of the mind; and were by nature the children of wrath, even as others (Ephesians 2:1-3).

That's what the Bible says about our former conversation (manner of life, behavior). It says other things as well, which are very specific about

our heart before we were saved. We would do well
to hear the Word, speak the Word, and read the
Word, for it will do more without a human counselor than any human counselor can do with
recycled Adlerian psychology. We would be better
off looking at Jesus, the author and finisher of our
faith, than looking into our past to discover a recycled style-of-life "key" to present transformation.

However, Bettler argues that simply putting off
ungodly behavior is not enough. A person may be
continuing his former manner of life in his
attempts to reach his goals. Thus, Jacob, according
to Bettler's analysis, might attempt to obey God in
his quest of getting ahead. A person could be
continuing his sinful manner of life ("gotta get
ahead") through obedience to God's commands.
Thus, for Bettler, biblical confrontation must go
below the surface, identify inner motivation, and
strike at the very heart of man. The old Adam
must be understood in terms of his manner of life,
dissembled piece by piece and repented of piece by
piece from the inside. If a counselor is necessary for
this type of inner work, he will have a "counselee"
for a long, long time.

Whereas Jay Adams has repeatedly taught the
importance of putting off sinful actions, attitudes,
thoughts and motivations, he has also repeatedly
shown that we, as humans, can only judge and
confront what is external in words and actions. He
leaves the inner work to God while confronting the
external sin. While he would encourage an individual to examine his own thoughts, attitudes, motivations and desires, we see no evidence in his

writings that he presumed to know them through some recycled psychological methodology. This is where Bettler and others at CCEF appear to go beyond the foundation which Adams laid. They try to go beneath the surface to reach into the depths of the inner man. Bettler's teaching about manner of life implies that God does not have the means to transform a person from darkness to light without the insights gleaned from Adler and other theorists who seek to peer into the soul and fix it from the inside out.

Since Scripture assigns this inner work to the Word of God and the Holy Spirit within the individual Christian, Bettler and others must go outside Scripture to find a psychological system that purports to do the inner work. This desire to devise a form of biblical counseling that will fix the inner man is what made Larry Crabb so appealing to CCEF. Although Bettler apparently disagrees with some aspects of Crabb's system, his own recycling bears similarities.

Two Tragedies

Two tragedies occur as Bettler attempts to use Scripture to support his recycled Adlerian teachings about using the past to discover a "counselee's" manner of life. First is the inevitable distortion of Scripture to support a psychological orientation. Second, the theory is presented as biblical when, in fact, it has been drawn from secular sources. Bettler presents his concept of manner of life as though he discovered it in Scripture, but the theory and practice which he attaches to those words come from Adlerian theory. Listeners not familiar with Adlerian theory may assume that Bettler found all these ideas in Scripture.

Bettler should have been up front about his use of Adlerian psychology. Since his teachings are an excellent example of recycling, he should have identified them as such, both for the sake of fairness and for the purpose of demonstrating how recycling works to supplement and interpret Scripture with the wisdom of men.

Bettler's doctrines of using the past to discover a person's manner of life (motivations, desires, attitudes, life goal, and means to that goal) did **not** come from careful biblical analysis, but from proof-texting with Adlerian notions. Therefore, Bettler should be saying how important recycling really is. After all, earlier in these teachings about the past, he declares:

> My point in a nutshell: **If you're going to do counseling, you've got to know the person's manner of life**, and when you talk about the past and the counselee talks about his past, your purpose is not to uncover history; your purpose is to uncover his *anastrophe*, his manner of life, the way he has processed all of those things that have happened to him and brought them into a **style of life**. (Emphasis added.)

If this is essential for good counseling, then Bettler should stress the importance of recycling, because without recycling he could never have come up with these teachings.

A *Hunting Expedition*

While Bettler emphasizes the importance of knowing someone's manner of life and gives examples of discovering a person's manner of life through his examples of Joseph and Jacob, he never really explains how to do it or reveals how much guesswork is involved in the process. Bettler simply says:

> When you uncover a person's history, when you look at his history, your purpose is not to get the facts—not that the facts aren't important (please don't misunderstand me)—but what you want to uncover is his *anastrophe*, his manner of life, and you want to see how that's being played out in the present.

In most instances the counselor who looks for a manner of life will discover the manner of life he is looking for, whether it's true or not, just as therapists using dream interpretation will find what they're looking for.

Looking for a person's style of life is a hunting expedition. This can be seen in case studies written by Adlerian therapists. Consistent in all of them is that the style of life is what the person does to reach his goal, such as "get ahead no matter what." The hunting expedition into an individual's past is fraught with subjective interpretation, speculation, and preconceived notions. How many counselors who listened to Bettler's teachings have since discovered at least one "counselee" with a "gotta get ahead" manner of life? How many have thought up other cryptic phrases to attach to their "counselees"? How many really know the inner manner of life they think they know?

There is no evidence in Scripture that people had to look into their past to learn how to live the Christian life. Jesus had set them free. Instead of examining the inner life style of fellow Christians, Paul simply contrasts what they were with what they are now:

> Know ye not that the unrighteous shall not inherit the kingdom of God? Be not deceived: neither fornicators, nor idolaters, nor adulterers, nor effeminate, nor abusers of themselves with mankind, nor thieves, nor covetous, nor drunkards, nor revilers, nor extortioners, shall inherit the kingdom of God. **And such were some of you: but ye are washed, but ye are sanctified, but ye are justified in the name of the Lord Jesus, and by the Spirit of our God** (1 Corinthians 6:9-11).

If details of those past life styles were important, if insight into each one's specific, unique past was essential for living the Christian life, there would be explicit directions. We would not have to search out secular theories and recycle them.

"Towards a 'Confession of Faith' on the Past"

Bettler ends his talk by reading through what he calls "a beginning statement of faith about what a person must believe about certain critical areas in counseling if he is to call himself biblical." This is CCEF's recently developed statement titled "Towards a 'Confession of Faith' on the Past," which has more than a taint of Bettler's Adlerian background and orientation. A repeated expression in this "Confession" is "manner of life." Another expression is "repentance for the distorted values and habits of a false 'manner of life.'" Why not use the word *sinful* or *sins*? The words *sin, sins,* and *sinful* are glaringly absent from the list. How can one even refer to a person's past without seeing the obvious and calling sin *sin*? Are these words out of date? Or not academic enough?

As mentioned earlier, Bettler's three talks titled "Dealing with a Person's Past" were also printed in the Winter, 1994, issue of *The Journal of Biblical Counseling*.[18] In a brief article in the July, 1993, issue of *The Biblical Counselor*, Bettler claims that the origin of the expression "manner of life" is Ephesians 4:22, "That ye put off concerning the former conversation the old man, which is corrupt according to the deceitful lusts."[19] As we indicated earlier, Bettler takes the words translated "former conversation" (KJV) and uses them to substantiate his "manner of life" theory.

The context of Ephesians 4:22 and the previous use of the word *conversation* in Ephesians 2:3 shows that the word *former* means pre-Christian, before a person is converted and given new life.

The word *conversation* could be translated "way of life," "behavior," or "conduct." Therefore, one could say that this refers to one's former manner of life.

However, when Better uses "manner of life" in the "Confession of Faith," he stresses the importance of exploring a "counselee's" past to find out how that person's inner "manner of life" developed. Bettler is looking for internal material relating to motivation and life goal, such as "gotta get ahead, no matter what." He tries to understand a Christian's present life by looking at the former internal "manner of life." The Adlerian content is so clear that almost every one of the items in the "Confession of Faith" list would be affirmed by an Adlerian. **Adlerians would see that Bettler's "manner of life" is really Adler's "style of life," recycled.**

Although the title appears to be a modest attempt at a tremendously difficult task, "**Towards** a 'Confession of Faith' on the Past," it seems strange that a 25-year-old institution that purports to teach and practice biblical counseling is just now deciding what constitutes biblical counseling. Worse than strange is the inclusion of material that was recycled from the wisdom of men and then presented as biblical. Yet there has been some confusion at CCEF over the years as to what biblical counseling really is.

The National Association of Nouthetic Counselors (NANC) published its newsletter with Bettler's article "Towards a 'Confession of Faith' on the Past." The article, though short, gave enough information to reveal Bettler's recycled use of

Adlerian psychology that it should have evoked a protest immediately after its publication. A call to the Executive Director of NANC, months after the appearance of the article, revealed there was not even one complaint. We think it fair to say that there has been wholesale acceptance of recycling, exemplified by Bettler's teachings on the past, among those who call themselves biblical counselors.

Committed to Recycling

CCEF is committed to recycling. Powlison conducted an interview with Adams and Bettler. During the interview, which appears in *The Journal of Biblical Counseling*, the idea of recycling came up. Adams says:

> What psychologists see about people might contribute out on the thinner edge of biblical teaching where we have general principles that need to be filled in. The large, central core of fundamental biblical principles is what's most important. It's hard to find one word to express what a biblical counselor should do out on that thinner edge. I applaud you in coming up with the word "recycle," John, but I still think the idea is hard to express in a word.[20]

Bettler responds:

> It's your word. . . . I presented the concept. I read some long sentence about the Christ-

ian's relationship to the behavioral sciences, that it was one of recognizing the antithesis, and then bringing out the distorted truths that must be reinterpreted from the Scriptures. I finished my sentence; and you said, "That was great, John. Why don't you use the word 'recycle'?"[21]

While this interview discussed the beginning of CCEF's use of the word *recycle* and the possibility of its use instead of other words such as *reinterpret* or *recast*, there was **no opposition** to the idea of recycling. During the interview, Adams says of Bettler's use of recycling: "I know what you mean and I agree with you."[22] Here are three individuals who are considered leaders in the biblical counseling movement agreeing on the idea of recycling.

In the same interview, Adams says of Bettler's teaching on the influence of the past:

He's incisive, and he has contributed things that are extremely helpful. Take his teaching this week on how to understand the influence of the past biblically. He stated things I've said, but much more clearly than I ever said them, sharpening and filling it out much more fully.[23]

Adams is referring to Bettler's three messages, "Dealing with a Person's Past," which we examined in this chapter. A later issue of *The Journal of Biblical Counseling* includes an article titled "Counseling and the Problem of the Past," which is based on

Bettler's same three lectures. In commenting on the article, Powlison says of Bettler, "He makes sense—biblical and practical sense—of the influence of the past."[24]

Bettler says at the beginning of his article:

> This article originated as a series of popular lectures delivered at a recent counseling conference sponsored by CCEF. The editor of this journal [David Powlison] had the lectures transcribed and edited them into this present form. He has successfully transposed them into written English without totally destroying the oral style.[25]

There is no question that Adams and Powlison support what Bettler says in those lectures and in the lengthy article transcribed and edited from the tapes.

On the other hand, we believe that, whether one calls it "integration" or "recycling," CCEF has fallen dramatically short of the biblical standard. One Bible college professor says:

> Recycling is not worth the risk or the image. The risk is that great mistakes can be made by the various people who recycle. And the image it conveys is that it looks suspiciously like integration.

In the Fall 1990 edition of the *Journal of Humanistic Psychology* there is an article titled "Alfred Adler's Influence on the Three Leading

Cofounders of Humanistic Psychology."[26] Perhaps someone should write an article titled "Alfred Adler's Influence on Biblical Counseling."

A Death Knell?

Again, this chapter simply gives examples of how counselors integrate psychology into their "biblical counseling," all the while thinking they are being faithful to the Lord and His Word. This revelation of recycling should demonstrate how easy it is to slip into psychological ways of understanding people and helping them change, even on the part of those who are leaders in the movement. This drift narrows the difference between biblical counselors and psychological integrationists. **Isn't it time to sound the death knell for "biblical counseling"?**

Let the apostles, prophets, evangelists, pastors, and teachers do the "perfecting of the saints for the work of the ministry, for the edifying of the body of Christ" (Ephesians 4:11-12). Those who wish to remain faithful to Scripture and the sufficiency of Christ should depart from much of what is now called "biblical counseling" and simply minister to one another in the mercy and grace of God without the title "biblical counselor." After all, Jesus Christ, the Holy Spirit, and the Word of God are our true counselors. We can come alongside one another, encourage and admonish, but we cannot perform the inner work in another person. We cannot even diagnose the difficulty beyond the plain words of Scripture.

7

For the Bible: Against Biblical Counseling

In thinking about how God has already given believers all they need to live the Christian life, we were reminded of a children's book that was read again and again in our house. It is a story about Little Bear, who wants to go out to play but complains about being too cold. Each time Little Bear comes in to complain about being cold, his mother makes him an additional piece of clothing. Finally she says, "My little bear, you have a hat, you have a coat, you have snow pants. Do you want a fur coat, too?" Mother Bear then removes the clothes she made for him and shows him his own fur coat. Little Bear is finally warm.[1] Christians do have all they need to live the Christian life. Nevertheless, they have loaded themselves with other problem-solving and self-improvement technologies.

Manual Mania

One of the main attractions of some biblical counseling programs is the manual approach. A manual can be a very handy reference and provide quick reference to Scriptures regarding particular sins and problems of living. It may be useful in applying Scriptures in one's own life and in ministering to others. A manual can be useful as a supplementary aid to be used along with concordances, Bible dictionaries, commentaries, and other Bible helps. However, we now have strong reservations about biblical counseling manuals as well as about biblical counseling training.

A type of manual mania occurs. The person who desires to minister to fellow believers is intimidated into believing he must master the manual before he can minister. In many cases the manual becomes the primary text, rather than the Bible itself. Using the manual seems to create confidence in the manual itself and can even encourage laziness with respect to learning the whole counsel of God. After all, it may be easier to use a manual than to study the whole Word of God, think it through, live by it, and trust the Lord's direct involvement with His Word. Counselors can become so dependent on the manual that removing it causes insecurity and even an inability to counsel.

The manual approach can also foster legalism. While it is possible to use the Bible in a legalistic fashion, it is doubly a danger with biblical counseling manuals because of their structure. Any manual with a discreet list of problem areas and a specified list of verses that must be studied to deal with the problem far more readily augers towards a legalistic approach.

Some manuals give the impression that the verse-after-verse-centered-around-a-problem approach is the best way to overcome sinful attitudes and actions and other problems of living. Yet, the Lord had a reason for organizing Scripture the way He did, instead of presenting lists of sayings organized by specific problems. Slicing Scripture and reorganizing verses according to specific problems may be one way to look at various problems, but the best way to study the Word of God and thereby grow spiritually (overcoming sinful attitudes and actions and other problems of living) is to read, study and obey verses as they were written—in sentences surrounded by other sentences within their context of meaning and application.

Such manuals tend towards focusing on problems instead of focusing on spiritual growth. They tend towards focusing on a multitude of isolated verses related to specific problems instead of learning the whole counsel of God. Many Christians believe that the only way to counsel is to know or have ready access to specific Bible verses related to specific sins and problems of life. While knowing verses regarding specific problems may be very helpful, such knowledge is not necessary if one knows the Lord, has studied the whole counsel of God, and has walked in obedience to the Lord. For example, a person confesses bitterness over an offense that occurred over ten years ago. Another could come alongside and minister by asking questions about when the offense occurred, how often the bitterness comes up, when the prior time was that the bitterness became overwhelming. One could take out a counselor's manual, look up all the verses under bitterness and minister them to the individual. However, none of the above is necessary.

The person is obviously spiritually stagnant and needs to be ministered to in such a way that the Holy Spirit convicts the heart and brings forth God's revelation about Himself and about the person who is bitter. It is only the Lord who can see the heart and change it. It is only the Lord who can bring forth the fruit of the Spirit. The person who comes alongside may be there to encourage the individual to search Scripture, to seek to know God's will in the matter, to examine his own heart to see what the Lord plans to change first. The person who comes alongside may be there to admonish or even console.

Believers are to fill themselves with the whole counsel of God for daily living. Then they are prepared for specific challenges in their own lives and for ministering God's wisdom and grace to one another. Rather than depending on a manual with its lists of verses, they have the Word written on their hearts so that the Holy Spirit can bring to mind what is needed in a particular situation. In this way the dependence is on God and His Word rather than on a manual.

Every situation is an opportunity to know God better. Instead of relying on a manual of verses, believers are to rely on the Lord. This is not a passive sort of reliance, but an active expectation to see God work His works according to His ways. Too often we are shortsighted regarding problems of living. We want to help people get over the problems, when God has a much bigger plan in mind, in which He is using the problem as a means of accomplishing that greater goal. Regarding this example of a Christian with bitterness—once the individual begins to know Christ better, to grow spiritually, and to reach a higher level of spiritual maturity, the bitterness will be dealt with as a consequence of spiritual growth, even if bitterness was barely addressed by the person who came alongside.

What some who counsel may not realize is that it is entirely unnecessary to use a manual or even to discuss the problem that led the person to seek counsel. Counsel using the Scripture and empowered by the Holy Spirit is effective whether or not one even discusses the problem. This is probably the most difficult idea to communicate to those who are dependent on a manual, method, or training program. **A believer empowered by the Holy Spirit and armed with Scripture never has and never will need a manual, method or training program!**
Another problem with the problem-centered, manual approach is the use of a personal data

intake form. Some are like those used by psychologists and give the impression that the questions and answers are important for counseling and that a professional evaluation will therefore be made. The need for a manual inspired, psychological replica is entirely unnecessary, puts the "counselee" in a one-down position, and often inhibits ministering spiritually to a person. Instead of the focus being on spiritual growth and personal responsibility, the questionnaire becomes a my-question-your-answer interchange that can quench the work of the Spirit and inadvertently shift responsibility for change to the "counselor."

Manuals are wonderful for technology. Formulas are necessary in chemistry. But the work of the Lord in an individual's life is beyond technology and will not conform to formulas. Therefore, we caution people to use biblical counseling manuals only as peripheral supplementation and then with discretion. A manual may be a supplementary tool, but it should not be used as a methodology for counseling.

God-Given Resources

By adding the wisdom of men and various techniques of counseling, Christians lose sight of their God-given resources. Thus, as we are asking people to reconsider this area of biblical counseling, we are only asking them to remove the man-made garments so that they see that Christ is their life (Colossians 3:4).

The Lord has given each believer garments for spiritual warfare—for overcoming temptation and living a life pleasing to God. In addition to the garments of protection, there is the shield of faith and the sword of the Spirit, which is the Word of God. In attempting to help fellow believers with problems of living, well-meaning Christians try to wield the sword of the Spirit with one hand and a man-made sword of the flesh with the other. Those who seek to counsel biblically often use psychological counseling theories and therapies for helps and tools, which they try to squeeze into "biblical categories."

Psychologists may attempt to study the soul through observing behavior and through speculating about the inner workings of individuals, but they cannot know the soul apart from the revelation of God. In short, the study of the soul apart from Scripture will be contaminated by the noetic effects of the Fall and by the fact that no one can see into another person's heart. Scripture is very clear about this.

Those who want to glean from psychology accuse pastors of dealing only with externals and accuse Christians of being superficial. However, the dangers inherent in making assumptions about an individual's inner man are even greater. Apart from the Holy Spirit and the Word of God, a person cannot take the internal spiritual temperature of himself. Apart from what Scripture says about the heart, no one can know what is going on inside another person. "For what man knoweth the things of a man, save the spirit of man which is in him? even so the things of God knoweth no man, but the Spirit of God" (1 Corinthians 2:11). Furthermore, in attempting to analyze another person's inner life, a counselor is in danger of usurping the place of the Lord and of leading a person astray with his speculation.

The Christian life is lived both internally and externally. Man works out what God works within. "Wherefore, my beloved, as ye have always obeyed, not as in my presence only, but now much more in my absence, work out your own salvation with fear and trembling. For it is God which worketh in you both to will and to do of his good pleasure" (Philippians 2:12,13).

People criticize some counseling approaches for being external and superficial. They are wanting to minister to the inner man, but in their desire to do so they have brought in foreign elements, such as Adler's *style of life*. But all such approaches are speculative, even if they sound right, because there is only one source for knowing the inner spiritual condition of a man. That source is the Lord. He reveals a person's inner man to that person alone, and He does so through the Bible (Hebrews 4:12), through the counsel of the Holy Spirit (John 14:16,17; 16:7-10), and through the knowledge of Christ (2 Peter 1:8). Any other source of understanding the inner man is either human speculation or demonic inspiration.

Where does that leave Christians? That should drive Christians to the very bosom of the Lord, who both died for them and lives in them. In some strange way, many of us forget that Jesus said, "I will never leave thee, nor forsake thee" (Hebrews 13:5). He is not just present with us, but lives in and through us by the Holy Spirit. Christ bought us with a price; we are not our own. We belong to Him. We are His. We are one with Him and one with the Father, just as He prayed (John 17). In all this search for self-identity through various psychological means, Christians have lost sight of the very presence of Jesus Christ in the believer.

New Creation in Christ

The Christian is not simply a person who has adopted a belief system. The Christian is a new creation: "Therefore if any man be in Christ, he is a new creature: old things are passed away; behold, all things are become new" (2 Corinthians 5:17). Christians are God's "workmanship, created in Christ Jesus unto good works, which God hath before ordained that we should walk in them" (Ephesians 2:10).

Trying to glean wisdom and practical helps from psychological counseling theories and therapies to help Christians live is utter foolishness. Christians are to live by the very life of Christ in them. What can atheists, secular humanists, and agnostics (the very enemies of Christ) say about His life in the believer? If the believer is living by any other life (i.e., the old self, which can only be what is still activated by the flesh), he is not to improve himself simply by changing habits or behavior; he needs to deny himself, stop living the self-life, and live by the very life of Christ.

Christians often try to follow Christ through a legalistic form of self effort. However, God has given each believer a new kind of life. The Christian is born again as a member of a different race. God is his Father. "But as many as received him, to them gave he power to become the sons of God, even to them that believe on his name: Which were born, not of blood, nor of the will of the flesh, nor of the will of man, but of God" (John 1:12,13). Because the Holy Spirit lives in believers, they are able to "put off concerning the former conversation the old man, which is corrupt according to the deceitful lusts" (Ephesians 4:22). Then, through the Holy Spirit's enabling, believers are called to "be renewed in the spirit of your mind and that ye put on the new man, which after God is created in righteousness and true holiness" (Ephesians 4:23,24).

The "new man" or "new self" is completely dependent upon Christ. The believer is to say as Jesus said: "Verily, verily, I say unto you, **The Son can do nothing of himself**, but what he seeth the Father do: for what things soever he doeth, these also doeth the Son likewise" (John 5:19). Jesus made very clear to His disciples this truth, which is essential for us today:

> Abide in me, and I in you. As the branch cannot bear fruit of itself, except it abide in the vine; no more can ye, except ye abide in me. I am the vine, ye are the branches: He that abideth in me, and I in him, the same bringeth forth much fruit: for **without me ye can do nothing** (John 15:4,5).

If the believer can do nothing without Christ, what is he trying to accomplish through vain philosophies and psychologies of men? They can describe nothing of Christ's life in the believer. Nor can they in any way therapize Christ in the believer. They can only work with the flesh. They may help a person develop external "virtues," but they cannot touch the essence of Christ, who is both Savior and Lord, living in the believer through the Holy Spirit.

How grievous that so many Christians are living at a subchristian level, trying to obey Christ through their own efforts. Then, when their own efforts fail, they try to obey through some kind of counseling that helps them fix up Old Adam. One does not have to investigate a person's "manner of life," for instance, to discover if a person is walking after the flesh. If one attempts to reveal the mistaken notions that have led to a particular manner of life, there is a strong possibility that the results will be the same as those Adler worked for: an improved life on the human plane, i.e., the Old Adam. And, as wonderful as putting off old habits and putting on new habits can be, unless such changes are wrought through Christ by faith, they are superficial and misleading dead works.

The heart change that must be continually made is "not I, but Christ." This is what Jesus meant when He said: "If any man will come after me, let him deny himself, and take up his cross, and follow me" (Matthew 16:24). Taking up one's cross and denying self is reckoning the old man dead by not energizing it with the flesh (Romans

6:11) and living by faith in Christ—"not I, but Christ." Paul said: "I am crucified with Christ: nevertheless I live; yet not I, but Christ liveth in me: and the life which I now live in the flesh I live by the faith of the Son of God, who loved me, and gave himself for me" (Galatians 2:20). Many people think this verse only applies to mature believers or very spiritual believers. They do not realize this **is** the Christian life! The Christian life is Christ living His life through earthen vessels. That is so amazing! That Christ would live in us! But that is exactly what He does.

Lest we begin to puff ourselves up because of the fact that the very God of the universe lives in us and through us, Paul reminds us that we are only containers of what is excellent: "But we have this treasure in earthen vessels, that the excellency of the power may be of God, and not of us" (2 Corinthians 4:7). Those who understand the beauty and the glory of Christ living in them are the most humble of all, because they see the great difference between Christ in them and what they are in themselves apart from Christ.

Paul referred to the mystery of "Christ in you, the hope of glory" (Colossians 1:27). Our lives should express the very presence of Christ—not our works or even our ministry, but His work in us and His ministry through us. Paul also emphasized that he depended not on his own righteousness, but on Christ's righteousness.

> Yea doubtless, and I count all things but loss
> for the excellency of the knowledge of Christ

Jesus my Lord: for whom I have suffered the loss of all things, and do count them but dung, that I may win Christ, and be found in him, not having mine own righteousness, which is of the law, but that which is through the faith of Christ, the righteousness which is of God by faith (Philippians 3:8-9).

Living by Faith

Many Christians do not have a full understanding of salvation. They trust Christ's death on the cross to pay for their sins so that they can look forward to heaven. But they do not trust His life in them for everyday living. Perhaps they fail to understand this aspect of salvation that comes from Christ's resurrection: "Christ in you, the hope of glory." Thus, while they trust Him for eternity, they look to themselves and their circumstances for help with present problems. They forget that the Christian life is to continue as it began—by faith:

As ye have therefore received Christ Jesus the Lord, so walk ye in him: Rooted and built up in him, and stablished in the faith, as ye have been taught, abounding therein with thanksgiving (Colossians 2:6,7).

Paul chided the Galatians for not continuing as they had begun:

O foolish Galatians, who hath bewitched you, that ye should not obey the truth, before whose eyes Jesus Christ hath been evidently set forth, crucified among you? This only would I learn of you, Received ye the Spirit by the works of the law, or by the hearing of faith? Are ye so foolish? having begun in the Spirit, are ye now made perfect by the flesh? (Galatians 3:1-3).

All believers need a dose of doctrine about who Christ is, what He has done, and how He enables each believer to live pleasing to God through His indwelling presence. Jesus Christ, the living Word of God, lives in each believer through the Holy Spirit. The written Word of God helps believers to see what He has accomplished and will accomplish in the believer through faith. That was the grand discovery of Luther: "The just shall live by faith!" Paul declared:

> For I am not ashamed of the gospel of Christ: for it is the power of God unto salvation to every one that believeth; to the Jew first, and also to the Greek. For therein is the righteousness of God revealed from faith to faith: as it is written, The just shall live by faith (Romans 1:16,17).

Those who are trying to live the Christian life on their own are likely to fall into legalism—religious works or psychotherapeutic works. There is one work for the believer. It is the work of faith. When Jesus was asked, "What shall we do, that we might work the works of God?" (John 6:28), Jesus said, "This is the work of God, that ye believe on him whom he hath sent" (John 6:29).

The importance of faith cannot be overestimated. It is essential. We are told in Hebrews that "without faith it is impossible to please him: for he that cometh to God must believe that he is, and that he is a rewarder of them that diligently seek him" (Hebrews 11:6). The faith is in God, in Christ, in the Holy Spirit, and in God's Word. Unfortunately, faith preachers have nearly destroyed the meaning of the word *faith*. They have mistakenly taught that faith is somehow connected with believing for what we want. In Scripture true faith is trusting God for what He wills and wants, not what I will and want. If one lives by faith, he subjects his own private will to the will of God as he implicitly trusts God, no matter what happens. The just live by faith in God to accomplish His will in His way, because faith in God trusts in God's goodness, mercy, justice, and righteousness, as well as in His sovereign power and wisdom.

Some believers feel even more defeated when someone suggests they need to trust the Lord more. They wonder how they can generate enough faith. But faith cannot be generated through self-effort or self-talk or self-anything. The Scripture is clear about how faith comes: "So then faith cometh by hearing, and hearing by the word of God" (Romans 10:17). That verse applies mainly to hearing and believing the Gospel. Then as Paul explains how people are saved he says: "For by grace are ye saved through faith; and that not of yourselves: it is the gift of God: not of works, lest any man should boast" (Ephesians 2:8,9). Believers are saved through the faith given to them, and then they are to live by the faith Christ continues to supply. Paul declared that believers live by the faith of Christ, rather than by an independent faith separated from His life within them, when he wrote: "**I live by the faith of the Son of God**, who loved me, and gave himself for me" (Galatians 2:20).

Faith becomes the predominant attitude as a person walks according to the Spirit and comes to know God more and more intimately. Peter began his second epistle with these words:

> Simon Peter, a servant and an apostle of Jesus Christ, to them that have obtained like precious faith with us through the righteousness of God and our Saviour Jesus Christ: Grace and peace be multiplied unto you through the knowledge of God, and of Jesus our Lord, according as his divine power hath given unto us all things that pertain unto life and godliness, through the knowledge of him that hath called us to glory and virtue: Whereby are given unto us exceeding great and precious promises: that by these ye might be partakers of the divine nature, having escaped the corruption that is in the world through lust (2 Peter 1:1-4).

Here true believers have obtained the same precious faith as that of the apostles, and they obtained it not through their own righteousness or self-effort in trying to believe, but rather "through the righteousness of God and our Saviour Jesus Christ." Then notice how grace and peace are multiplied: "through the knowledge of God, and of Jesus our Lord." All that believers have in the Christian life is of God and from God. Believers can trust God's promises because He is trustworthy. His Word is true and He is faithful even when circumstances may indicate otherwise.

As you read this, you may be saying to yourself, "Oh, I've heard all that before. That is just elementary doctrine. Everyone knows that." But, if that is so, why are we not all living by these truths? Why are people looking for answers elsewhere? Could it be lack of obedience to what they know? Jesus told the parable of the wise person who was building a house:

> Whosoever cometh to me, and heareth my sayings, and doeth them, I will show you to whom he is like: He is like a man which built an house, and digged deep, and laid the foundation on a rock: and when the flood arose, the stream beat vehemently upon that house, and could not shake it: for it was founded upon a rock. But he that heareth, and doeth not, is like a man that without a foundation built an house upon the earth; against which the stream did beat vehemently, and immediately it fell; and the ruin of that house was great (Luke 6:47-49).

James continued the same essential doctrine when he wrote:

> But be ye doers of the word, and not hearers only, deceiving your own selves. For if any be a hearer of the word, and not a doer, he is like unto a man beholding his natural face in a glass: For he beholdeth himself, and goeth his way, and straightway forgetteth what manner of man he was. But whoso looketh into the perfect law of liberty, and continueth therein, he being not a forgetful hearer, but a doer of the work, this man shall be blessed in his deed (James 1:22-25).

As we obey what we know, the Lord reveals Himself more and more. Jesus explained:

> He that hath my commandments, and keepeth them, he it is that loveth me: and he that loveth me shall be loved of my Father, and I will love him, and will manifest myself to him . . . If a man love me, he will keep my words: and my Father will love him, and we will come unto him, and make our abode with him (John 14:21,23).

What wealth there is in Christ indwelling the believer! What untold supply is available through the Word of God! Christians have been spelunking in the caves of men's wisdom, hoping to find treasure, when all along the real treasure has been right before their eyes in the Word of God and right within their hearts (if they are true believers). "And God is able to make all grace abound toward you; that ye, always having all sufficiency in all things, may abound to every good work" (2 Corinthians 9:8).

Knowing Christ

The apostle John defined eternal life this way: "And this is life eternal, that they might know thee the only true God, and Jesus Christ, whom thou hast sent" (John 17:3). Oh that we might know Him more! That was Paul's great desire:

> I count all things but loss for the excellency of the knowledge of Christ Jesus my Lord. . . that I may know him, and the power of his resurrection, and the fellowship of his sufferings, being made conformable unto his death (Philippians 3:8,10).

The question is this: are we willing to "count all things but loss for the excellency of the knowledge of Christ Jesus"? Are we willing to give up our own ways so that the Holy Spirit will no longer be quenched and squeezed into our own agenda?

The Christian life cannot be earned or bought with worldly means. However, once we are saved we know that we have been bought with the precious blood of Jesus Christ and that we no longer have the right to own ourselves. "What? know ye not that your body is the temple of the Holy Ghost which is in you, which ye have of God, and ye are not your own? For ye are bought with a price:

therefore glorify God in your body, and in your spirit, which are God's" (1 Corinthians 6:19-20).

Rather than know ourselves better, we all need to know God better. Rather than focusing on trying to discover our self-identity, we need to know Him who lives in us both to will and do His own good purpose. We need to know Christ intimately through sound doctrine and obedience. We will not become more like Christ by examining ourselves or discovering our former "manner of life." The Bible says that we become more like Christ by looking at Him: "But we all, with open face beholding as in a glass the glory of the Lord, are changed into the same image from glory to glory, even as by the Spirit of the Lord" (2 Corinthians 3:18). Therefore, instead of looking selfward through biblical counseling recycled from the garbage of psychotherapy, believers are called to look Christward:

> Wherefore seeing we also are compassed about with so great a cloud of witnesses, let us lay aside every weight, and the sin which doth so easily beset us, and let us run with patience the race that is set before us, looking unto Jesus the author and finisher of our faith; who for the joy that was set before him endured the cross, despising the shame, and is set down at the right hand of the throne of God. For consider him that endured such contradiction of sinners against himself, lest ye be wearied and faint in your minds. Ye have not yet resisted unto blood, striving against sin (Hebrews 12:1-4).

A Challenge for Change

Most Bible colleges and seminaries teach psychology in a supportive way. We are utterly opposed to that. However, the answer to getting rid of psychology is not to replace it with biblical counseling. The answer is to teach the Bible. We wonder what goes on in theology and Bible classes when pastors graduate from seminary and cannot provide care for their sheep without taking special classes in psychology or biblical counseling. The message being communicated is this: studying theology and the Bible in present-day seminaries evidently does not prepare evangelists, pastors, and teachers "for the perfecting of the saints, for the work of the ministry, for the edifying of the body of Christ: till we all come in the unity of the faith, and of the knowledge of the Son of God, unto a perfect man, unto the measure of the stature of the fulness of Christ" (Ephesians 4:12,13).

As we have already indicated, we are strongly opposed to biblical counseling outside the church and we are opposed to biblical counseling as a separate ministry in the church. We are also opposed to any biblical counseling that is merely a reflection of psychological counseling, whether it is in or out of the church. On the other hand, we do favor and support the use of biblical counsel that is part of the ministries and callings established by Scripture, which includes the priesthood of all believers.

We back away from the terms *counseling, counselor,* and *counselee* because they are too strongly rooted in a socio-cultural mind-set and are too much a part of the psychotherapeutic mentality. Some terms become too corrupted and too imbued with meanings that are foreign to the Bible to be used. We confess that we have used those words throughout our writings. Someday the church may also have to back away from these terms, either because of counseling certification requirements by the state or to protect the church from malpractice lawsuits having to do with counseling.

Though we stand by much of what we taught in our book *How to Counsel from Scripture*, we repent from certain aspects of the book that were influenced by the therapeutic community. For instance, we would no longer call the biblical doctrine of man a "biblical model of man." We would certainly back away from calling the change wrought by faith and obedience through the enabling of the Holy Spirit "a biblical methodology of change." The Bible and the Holy Spirit are God's truth and power for transformation—not a model or methodology of change. We would no longer wish to develop and promote the roles of "counselor and counselee." In our chapter "A Plan for Counseling in Your Church," we took biblical principles and molded them into a twentieth-century format to provide a replacement for psychological counseling. We believe now that we encouraged a therapeutic mentality and gave credence to a technology of change. **Therefore, our criticism of biblical counseling includes ourselves.**

We are concerned about the growing popularity of the biblical counseling movement, and we doubt that this book will stop the trend. It is as though biblical counseling has become a life raft in the sea of psychobabble, psychotechniques, and psychoheresy. And the life raft crowd is working hard at making their craft appealing to those who are floating along on the flotsam of psychology. Nevertheless, the biblical counseling raft continues to be tossed to and fro in that sea of psychoheresy. Thus we encourage believers to get out of the sea and stand on the solid rock. Believers do not need what the world offers or any facsimile thereof.

While we have moved away from biblical counseling, others are setting their sails and hoping to increase their size and influence. A Special Edition of *Pulse* reports a new direction for the Christian Counseling and Educational Foundation (CCEF). The headline reads: "CCEF to Invest $500,000 in Growth of Biblical Counseling." The article begins by saying:

> In October of 1993, CCEF quietly launched the most significant undertaking of its 25 year history. *LAUNCH 2000* is a $500,000 capital campaign which will enable CCEF to propel the message of distinctly biblical counseling around the world. The demand for our educational programs here and abroad has out-distanced our resources.[2]

The Biblical Counseling Foundation's *Self-Confrontation Syllabus for Course 1: Biblical Counseling Training Program*, while originally published by BCF, is now being published by Thomas Nelson Publishers.[3] We were told that Nelson is publishing it because they see a large potential market for it. Nelson also publishes some of the most flagrantly psychological books in the Christian market. And, just like its CCEF counterpart, BCF is attempting to raise the same amount of money for a similar purpose. A letter from BCF says:

> We in BCF see the hunger firsthand of many overseas Christian leaders for Bible-centered materials that will help them train believers to face and deal with every problem and circumstance of life. The door is wide open.
>
> The projected cost of Discipleship 2000 is $500,000 over the next 18 months.[4]

Training counselors has been a high priority for CCEF, BCF, and other biblical counseling groups. We question the validity of training that is especially geared to counseling for several reasons. (1) There is a tendency to emulate the world both in confirming authority through training and in adding techniques "recycled" from psychological counseling. (2) Those who are not "trained" as counselors will be fearful of ministering to fellow believers. (3) Training may give a "biblical counselor" a false sense of confidence and therein bypass full dependence on the Lord. (4) The real training for giving counsel is training in the doctrines of Scripture.

> Study to show thyself approved unto God, a workman that needeth not to be ashamed,

rightly dividing the word of truth. But shun profane and vain babblings: for they will increase unto more ungodliness (2 Timothy 2:15,16).

Those who have been studying the Word and obeying it through faith over a period of time are better equipped to minister than those who have taken a course, especially if the course includes any of the "vain babblings" of psychology. (5) Some of the most important requirements for ministering to one another in the body of Christ cannot be taught, such as love, joy, peace, longsuffering, gentleness, faith, hope, and compassion.

This appears to be a time of world-wide expansion for the biblical counseling movement. It would be a time when we would be more popular if we continued to recommend biblical counseling. **However, for all the reasons presented in this book, we can no longer encourage, support, or participate in the biblical counseling movement.**

Rather than embracing such contrived ministries as biblical counseling, it is time for Christians—pastors, teachers, elders and the priesthood of all believers—to be about the work of the Lord by emphasizing the true biblical ministries of the church as outlined in Ephesians 4 and Romans 12. The church did without both psychology and the biblical counseling movement for almost 2000 years.

At times the horrific errors in biblical counseling are much worse than those in psychological counseling. For instance, the errors of regressive therapy can become much worse in the hands of "biblical counselors" who perform so-called inner healing, which combines the worst of Freud and Jung with occult visualization, which often creates *another* Jesus as a spirit guide. We also think the errors at CCEF are very serious, though in a different direction. When biblical counselors at CCEF turn the Bible into categories, in which to place human notions and even vain philosophies, they are denying that the Word of God is complete. They are saying that the Bible has categories for adding human wisdom (i.e., "style of life") and psychological techniques (i.e., personality tests) to accomplish its work. But the Bible is clear about unequal yoking:

> Be ye not unequally yoked together with unbelievers: for what fellowship hath righteousness with unrighteousness? and what communion hath light with darkness? And what concord hath Christ with Belial? or what part hath he that believeth with an infidel? (2 Corinthians 6:14,15).

Adding notions of Adler and others constitutes unequal yoking of the Word of God with the speculations of godless men. The guard against these errors is to return once more to the true vine to receive the true fruit of the Spirit, instead of secular counterfeits or counterfeits in biblical garb.

On the other hand, we believe that there are biblical counselors who are ministering according to the Word of God who will be willing to examine what they are doing and move closer to a biblical ministry. They will encourage one another to return to the doctrines of Scripture, to think about them seriously and prayerfully, and then to live by them through the indwelling life of Christ. For some, there will be very little need for change, especially if they are not practicing the "onerous ones" mentioned earlier, if they are faithful to Scripture, and if they are part of the biblically ordained ministries, rather than apart from them. We would encourage them to help lead the church away from its love of counseling and into a love for the Lord and His Word.

Christ is sufficient. His "divine power hath given unto us all things that pertain unto life and godliness" (2 Peter 1:3). We don't need the "counselor," "counselee," and conversation of a contrived ministry called "biblical counseling." Thus, we encourage all Christians to be like the Bereans "in that they received the word with all readiness of mind, and searched the Scriptures daily, whether those things were so" (Acts 17:11).

There is some good that can be found in the teachings of NANC, BCF, and other organizations. However, the practice of the Onerous Ones and the multiplicity of errors of a biblical counseling ministry separated externally or internally from the biblically ordained ministries of the church are too multitudinous for us to recommend any of these organizations or biblical counseling programs.

Yes, we are against biblical counseling, but we are for the Bible, which gives us truth. We are for the Holy Spirit and His gifts of ministry (Ephesians 4:11-12; Romans 12:6-8). We are for Christians ministering to one another. The body of Christ already has all it needs to do what it is called to do. It just has to take off the garments of the world. Believers have all they need to live godly lives, because they have the Word of God and the Lord Jesus lives in them through the Holy Spirit.

A church does not need to have a "counseling ministry" or a counselor training program for believers to minister to one another according to Scripture. After all, what did believers do for almost 2000 years without the biblical counseling movement? There has been some personal care among believers ministering to one another through encouragement, admonition, discernment, comfort, counsel, compassion, prayer, and discipleship. This happened among believers from the inception of the church, because people believed and acted according to the Word of God, by the very life of Christ living in and through them by the Holy Spirit.

For years people have thought of biblical counseling as an alternative to psychological counseling. But, psychotherapy began as a religious alternative to Christianity. Therefore, rather than offering an alternative "look alike," we urge Christians to return to the Bible. Counsel from the Bible is not an alternative. It is God's truth versus the counsel of the world. It is God's light rather than the darkness of the wisdom of men. We call Christians back to the light of God's Word and the life of Christ in the believer.

The biblical counseling movement as it currently exists must die. . . . Is there any hope for the biblical counseling movement? Yes, but only resurrected in its proper place as a part of the biblically ordained ministries of the church. Instead of a "counseling" ministry Christians should follow the Bible regarding mutual care among believers, under biblically ordained leadership. The answer to problems of living is not biblical counseling, but ongoing biblical ministry in the body of Christ:

> Till we all come in the unity of the faith, and of the knowledge of the Son of God, unto a perfect man, unto the measure of the stature of the fulness of Christ: That we henceforth be no more children, tossed to and fro, and carried about with every wind of doctrine, by the sleight of men, and cunning craftiness, whereby they lie in wait to deceive; But speaking the truth in love, may grow up into him in all things, which is the head, even Christ: From whom the whole body fitly joined together and compacted by that which every joint supplieth, according to the effectual working in the measure of every part, maketh increase of the body unto the edifying of itself in love (Ephesians 4:13-16).

NOTES

Chapter 1: *Is Biblical Counseling Biblical?*

1. Martin and Deidre Bobgan. *The Psychological Way / The Spiritual Way*. Minneapolis: Bethany House Publishers, 1979.
2. Charles Bridges. *Exposition of the Book of Proverbs*. Carlisle, PA: Banner of Truth, 1846, 1968, p. 593.

Chapter 2: *Biblical Counseling and the Cure of Souls*

1. John T. McNeill. *A History of The Cure of Souls*. New York; Harper & Row, Publishers, 1951, p. vii.
2. *Ibid.*, pp. 89-96.
3. Quoted by McNeill, *ibid.*, p. 100.
4. McNeill, *ibid.*, p. 113.
5. *Ibid.*, p. 114.
6. *Ibid.*, p. 161.
7. *Ibid.*, p. 123.
8. E. Brooks Holifield. *A History of Pastoral Care In America: From Salvation to Self-Realization*. Nashville: Abingdon Press, 1983, p. 17.
9. McNeill, *op. cit.*, p. 142.
10. *Ibid.*, p. 161.
11. John Calvin quoted by McNeill, *ibid.*, p. 197.
12. Huldreich Zwingli. *On True and False Religion*, quoted by McNeill, *ibid.*, p. 196.
13. Richard Baxter. *Baxter's Practical Works, Vol. 1: A Christian Directory* (1673). Ligonier, PA: Soli Deo Gloria Publications, Reprint 1990.
14. Holifield, *op. cit.*, p. 23.
15. *Ibid.*, pp. 62-64.
16. *Ibid.*, p. 27.
17. *Ibid.*
18. *Ibid.*, p. 29.
19. *Ibid.*, pp. 87-88.
20. *Ibid.*, p. 90.
21. L. Berkhof. *Systematic Theology*. Grand Rapids: William B. Eerdmans Publishing Co., 1939, 1941, pp. 19-20.
22. J. B. Webster in *New Dictionary of Theology*, Sinclair Ferguson, David Wright, and J. I. Packer, eds. Downers Grove: InterVarsity Press, 1988, p. 620.
23. Holifield, *op. cit.*, pp. 131-134,140.

24. Robert C. Fuller. *Mesmerism and the American Cure of Souls.* Philadelphia: University of Pennsylvania Press, 1982, p. 10.
25. *Ibid.*, p. 12.
26. *Ibid.*, p. xii.
27. Thomas Szasz. *The Myth of Psychotherapy.* Garden City: Doubleday/Anchor Press, 1978, p. 43.
28. Mark Noll et al, eds. *Eerdman's Handbook to Christianity in America.* Grand Rapids: William B. Eerdman's Publishing Company, 1983, pp. 321-324.
29. James Turner. *Without God, Without Creed.* Baltimore: The Johns Hopkins University Press, 1985, p. xiii.
30. Holifield, *op. cit.*, p. 198.
31. William James. *The Will to Believe and Other Essays in Popular Philosophy* (1897). New York: Dover Publications, 1956, p. 120.
32. Holifield, *op. cit.*, pp. 204-208.
33. Gordon H. Clark. *Thales to Dewey.* Jefferson, MD: The Trinity Foundation, 1957, 1985, p. 528.
34. Holifield, *op. cit.*, p. 211.
35. John Lofton, "Norman Vincent Peale's Preaching is a Perfect Example of Savorless Salt Unfit for the Dunghill." *The Lofton Letter*, January 1994, p. 1.
36. Holifield, *op. cit.*, p. 221.
37. *Ibid.*, p. 271.
38. *The NAMH Program - How We Serve.* New York: National Association for Mental Health, Inc., 1965, p. 19.
39. P. Sutherland and P. Poelstra, "Aspects of Integration." Paper presented at the meeting of the Christian Association for Psychological Studies, Santa Barbara, CA, June, 1976.
40. Clyde M. Narramore. *The Psychology of Counseling.* Grand Rapids: Zondervan, 1960, p. 174.
41. Tim Stafford, "His Father's Son." *Christianity Today*, April 22, 1988, p. 20.
42. Jay E. Adams. *Ready to Restore.* Phillipsburg, NJ: Presbyterian and Reformed Publishing Co., 1981, p. 15.
43. Jay E. Adams. *Update on Christian Counseling*, Vol. 1 and 2. Grand Rapids: Zondervan, 1977, 1979, 1981, Introduction to Vol. 2.
44. Martin and Deidre Bobgan, *Prophets of PsychoHeresy I*, Santa Barbara: EastGate Publishers, 1989, Part II.
45. Special Advertising Section. *Christianity Today*, May 17, 1993, p. 60.
46. Frank Minirth, "Someone to Talk To." *Today's Better Life*, June/July 1994, pp. 42,43.
47. *Ibid.*, p. 44.

48. McNeill, *op. cit.*, p. 104.
49. *Ibid.*, p. 115.
50. Baxter, *op. cit.*, p. 403.
51. Holifield, *op. cit.*, p. 65.
52. Adams, *op cit.*, Introduction to Vol. 2.

Chapter 3: *Biblical Counseling and the Bible*
1. Mary Kay Blakely, "Psyched Out," *Los Angeles Times Magazine*, October 3, 1993, p. 28.
2. "Psychotherapists by the Numbers." *Common Boundary*, Jan/Feb 1994, p. 36.
3. Bernie Zilbergeld. *The Shrinking of America*. Boston: Little, Brown and Company, 1983, p. 32.
4. Martin Gross. *The Psychological Society*. New York: Random House, 1978, p. 3.
5. *The Words of the Old Testament*, Vol. 1. R. Laird Harris et al, eds. Chicago: Moody, 1980, p. 390.
6. *Matthew Henry's Commentary in One Volume*. Grand Rapids: Regency Reference Library, Zondervan Publishing House, 1960, p. 91.

Chapter 4: *The Onerous Ones*
1. Jay Haley. *Strategies of Psychotherapy*. New York: Grune & Stratton, Inc., 1963, pp. 183-184.
2. Alvin Sanoff, "Psychiatry Runs Into an Identity Crisis." *U.S. News and World Report*, October 9, 1978, p. 63.
3. Millard J. Sall. *Faith, Psychology and Christian Maturity*. Grand Rapids: Zondervan Publishing House, 1975, 1977, p. 13.
4. Martin and Deidre Bobgan. *PsychoHeresy: The Psychological Seduction of Christianity*. Santa Barbara: EastGate Publishers, 1987.
5. Ruth Matarazzo, "Research on the Teaching and Learning of Psychotherapeutic Skills." *Handbook of Psychotherapy and Behavior Change: An Empirical Analysis*. Allen Bergin and Sol Garfield, eds. New York: Wiley, 1971, p. 910.
6. Leslie Vernick, "Getting to the Heart of the Matter in Marriage Counseling." *The Journal of Biblical Counseling*, Vol. XII, Number 3, Spring 1994, pp. 31-35.
7. *Pulse.*, Fall 1993, p. 3.
8. Letter on file.

Chapter 5: *Biblical Counseling Compromise*
1. Gary Collins. *Psychology and Theology: Prospects for Integration*. Nashville: Abingdon, 1981, p. 15.

2. John Carter and Bruce Narramore. *The Integration of Psychology and Theology.* Grand Rapids: Zondervan Publishing House, 1979.

3. *Utne Reader*, May/April, 1987, p. 30.

4. Charles Tart. *Transpersonal Psychologies.* New York: Harper & Row, Publishers, 1975, p. 4.

5. John Bettler, "The Ivy Won't Have Time to Grow." *Pulse*, Winter-Spring 1993, p. 1.

6. Two Critiques on the Christian Counseling and Educational Foundation by Martin and Deidre Bobgan are available through PsychoHeresy Awareness Ministries, 4137 Primavera Road, Santa Barbara, CA 93110.

7. See Martin and Deidre Bobgan. *Four Temperaments, Astrology & Personality Testing.* Santa Barbara: EastGate Publishers, 1992, Chapters 8-10.

8. Christian Counseling and Educational Foundation 1991 Catalog, p. 6.

9. Christian Counseling and Educational Foundation 1987 Catalog, p. 28.

10. See Bobgan, *op. cit.*.

11. See Martin and Deidre Bobgan. *Prophets of PsychoHeresy I.* Santa Barbara: EastGate Publishers, 1989, Part 2.

12. *Pulse*, Vol. 5, No. 1, Winter 1987, p. 3.

13. *Pulse*, Vol. 6, No. 1, Winter 1988, p. 3.

14. Jay E. Adams in Bobgan, *Prophets of PsychoHeresy I, op. cit.*, p. 106.

15. *Pulse*, Vol. 6, No. 4, Fall 1988, p. 3.

16. Paul Vitz, "Christianity and Psychoanalysis (Parts One and Two): Jesus As The Anti-Oedipus." *Journal of Psychology and Theology*, Vol. 12, No. 1, 1984.

17. Vitz in *The Christian Vision: Man in Society.* Lynne Morris, ed. Hillsdale: The Hillsdale College Press, 1989, p. 80.

18. John Bettler, "Power Struggles in the Family, Part 2." Audio tape from the National Association of Nouthetic Counselors Conference, Fall 1991.

19. Bobgan, *Prophets of PsychoHeresy I, op. cit.*, Part Two.

20. Bettler, "Power Struggles in the Family, Part 2," *op. cit.*

21. Bobgan, *Prophets of PsychoHeresy I, op. cit.*

22. C. G. Jung. *Memories, Dreams, Reflections.* Aniela Jaffe, ed: Richard and Clara Winston, trans. New York: Pantheon, 1963, p. 183. (see also pp. 170-199).

23. Ed Welch, "Personality." Audio tape from CCEF East Summer Institute, 1987.

24. Jay E. Adams. *The Language of Counseling and the Christian Counselor's Wordbook.* Grand Rapids: Zondervan, 1981, p. 1.

25. Detailed critique on Leslie Vernick's article "When Sexually Abused Children Grow Up, What Do the Scriptures Say to Them?" is included in a critique on the Christian Counseling and Educational Foundation. The critique, written by Martin and Deidre Bobgan, is available through PsychoHeresy Awareness Ministries, 4137 Primavera Road, Santa Barbara, CA 93110.

26. "Does Your Childhood Abuse Still Hurt?" *Pulse*, Fall 1990, p. 3.

27. Jay E. Adams. *Essays on Counseling*. Grand Rapids: Zondervan, 1972, pp. 237ff.

28. See Martin and Deidre Bobgan. *12 Steps to Destruction*. Santa Barbara, CA: EastGate Publishers, 1991.

29. David Powlison, "Crucial Issues in Contemporary Biblical Counseling." *Journal of Pastoral Practice*, Vol. 9, No. 3 (1988), p. 76.

30. *Ibid.*, p. 77.

31. David Powlison, "Which Presuppositions? Secular Psychology and the Categories of Biblical Thought." *Journal of Psychology and Theology*. Vol. 12, No. 4, 1984, p. 272.

32. *Ibid.*, p. 277-278.

33. Lawrence Crabb, Jr. *Understanding People*. Grand Rapids: Zondervan Publishing House, 1987, pp. 66-73.

34. Bobgan. *Prophets of PsychoHeresy I, op. cit.*, Part 2.

35. Powlison, "Which Presuppositions?" *op. cit.*, p. 275.

36. Michael Scott Horton, ed. *Power Religion*. Chicago: Moody Press, 1992, jacket cover.

37. *Ibid.*

38. David Powlison, "Integration or Inundation," *Power Religion*, *ibid.*, p. 212.

39. *Ibid.*, p. 213.

40. Letter on file.

41. Tim Stafford, "How Christian Psychology is Changing the Church." *Christianity Today*, May 17, 1993, p. 26.

42. *Ibid.*, p. 32.

43. Robert C. Roberts, "Psychobabble." *Christianity Today*, May 16, 1994, p. 24.

44. *Ibid.*

45. David Powlison interviewed by Tim Stafford, "Needs and Idols." *Christianity Today*, May 17, 1993, p. 21.

46. "How to Choose a Counselor." *Christianity Today*, May 17, 1993, p. 59.

47. *Ibid.*

48. *Ibid.*, p. 65.

49. "Christian Counseling Directory." *Christianity Today*, May 16, 1994, p. 68.
50. *Ibid.*, p. 71.

Chapter 6: Recycling or Integration?
1. "Counseling Methodologies" (CC44), Christian Counseling and Educational Foundation Catalog, 1991.
2. *Ibid.*
3. Letter on file.
4. John Bettler, "Towards a 'Confession of Faith' in the Past." *The Biblical Counselor*, July 1993, p. 3.
5. John Bettler, "Counseling and the Problem of the Past." *The Journal of Biblical Counseling*, Winter, 1994, pp. 5-23.
6. John Bettler, "Dealing with a Person's Past." Audio tapes from the CCEF 1993 Summer Institute. Michigan City, IN: Sound Word Associates, Tapes 9305-9307.
7. B. H. Shulman, "Adlerian Psychology." *Encyclopedia of Psychology*. Raymond J. Corsini, ed. New York: John Wiley and Sons, 1984, p. 18.
8. Calvin Hall and Gardner Lindzey. *Theories of Personality*. New York: John Wiley and Sons, 1957, pp. 120-123.
9. *Ibid.*, p. 124.
10. *Ibid.*, p. 125.
11. *Ibid.*, p. 124.
12. Alfred Adler, "The Fundamental Views of Individual Psychology," *International Journal of Individual Psychology*, 1935, p. 5.
13. See Martin and Deidre Bobgan. *Prophets of PsychoHeresy I*. Santa Barbara: EastGate Publishers, 1989, Part 2.
14. Hall & Lindzey, *op cit.*, pp. 123-125.
15. Alfred M. Freedman, Harold I. Kaplan, Benjamin J. Sadock. *Modern Synopsis of Comprehensive Textbook of Psychiatry / II*, Second Edition. Baltimore: The Williams & Wilkins Co., 1976, p. 278.
16. Dorothy E. Peven and Bernard H. Shulman, "Adlerian Therapy." *Psychotherapist's Casebook: Theory and Technique in the Practice of Modern Therapies*. Irwin Kutash and Alexander Wolf, eds. Northvale, NJ: Jason Aronson Inc., 1986, pp. 109, 118, 122.
17. Alfred Adler. *The Pattern of Life*. W. Beran Wolfe, ed. London: Kegan Paul, Trench Trubner & Co, Ltd., 1931, p.41.
18. Bettler, "Counseling and the Problem of the Past," *op. cit.*, pp. 5-23.
19. Bettler, "Towards a 'Confession of Faith' in the Past," *op. cit.*, p. 3.

20. Jay Adams in "25 Years of Biblical Counseling." *The Journal of Biblical Counseling*, Fall 1993, p. 11.
21. *Ibid*., pp. 11-12.
22. *Ibid*. p. 11.
23. *Ibid*., p. 12.
24. David Powlison, "From the Editor's Desk: Do You Use This Journal?" *The Journal of Biblical Counseling*, Winter 1994, p. 4.
25. Bettler, "Counseling and the Problem of the Past," *op. cit.*, p. 5.
26. Heinz L. Ansbacher, "Alfred Adler's Influence on the Three Leading Cofounders of Humanistic Psychology," *Journal of Humanistic Psychology*, Vol. 30, No. 4, Fall 1990, pp. 45-53.

Chapter 7: For the Bible: Against Biblical Counseling

1. Else Holmelund Minarik. *Little Bear*. New York: Harper-Collins Publishers, 1957, 1985.
2. "CCEF to Invest $500,000 in Growth of Biblical Counseling." *Pulse*, Vol. 12, No. 2, Spring 1994, p. 1.
3. John C. Broger et al. *Self-Confrontation: A Manual for In-Depth Discipleship*. Nashville: Thomas Nelson Publishers, 1994.
4. Biblical Counseling Foundation Letter, May 2, 1994.

OTHER BOOKS FROM EASTGATE

Competent to Minister: The Biblical Care of Souls by Martin and Deidre Bobgan encourages believers to care for one another in the Body of Christ and demonstrates that God enables them to do so without incorporating the methods of the world. Contains much practical information for developing personal care ministries within the local fellowship of believers. Topics include overcoming obstacles to caring for souls, salvation and sanctification, caring for souls inside and out, ministering mercy and truth, caring for one another through conversation and practical helps, cautions to heed in caring for souls. This book exposes the professional, psychological intimidation that has discouraged Christians from ministering to one another during trials and temptations. It both encourages and reveals how God equips believers to minister to one another.

Four Temperaments, Astrology & Personality Testing by the Bobgans answers such questions as: Do the four temperaments give valid information? Are there biblically or scientifically established temperament or personality types? Are personality inventories and tests valid ways of finding out about people? How are the four temperaments, astrology, and personality testing connected? Personality types and tests are examined from a biblical, historical, and research basis.

Christian Psychology's War On God's Word: The Victimization Of The Believer by Jim Owen is about the sufficiency of Christ and how "Christian" psychology undermines believers' reliance on the Lord. Owen demonstrates how "Christian" psychology pathologizes sin and contradicts biblical doctrines of man. He further shows that "Christian" psychology treats people more as victims needing psychological intervention than sinners needing to repent. Owen beckons believers to turn to the all-sufficient Christ and to trust fully in His ever-present provisions, the power of His indwelling Holy Spirit, and the sure guidance of the inerrant Word of God.

OTHER BOOKS FROM EASTGATE

The End of "Christian Psychology" by Martin and Deidre Bobgan discusses research about the question,"Does psychotherapy work?" analyzes why Christians use psychological counseling, and gives evidence showing that professional psychotherapy with its underlying psychologies is questionable at best, detrimental at worst, and a spiritual counterfeit at least. The book includes descriptions and analyses of major psychological theorists and reveals that "Christian psychology" involves the same problems and confusions of contradictory theories and techniques as secular psychology. This book presents enough biblical and scientific evidence to shut down both secular and "Christian psychology."

PsychoHeresy: The Psychological Seduction of Christianity by Martin and Deidre Bobgan exposes the fallacies and failures of psychological counseling theories and therapies for one purpose: to call the Church back to curing souls by means of the Word of God and the work of the Holy Spirit rather than by man-made means and opinions. Besides revealing the anti-Christian biases, internal contradictions, and documented failures of secular psychotherapy, *PsychoHeresy* examines various amalgamations of secular psychologies with Christianity and explodes firmly entrenched myths that undergird those unholy unions.

12 Steps to Destruction: Codependency/Recovery Heresies by the Bobgans provides information for Christians about codependency/recovery teachings, Alcoholics Anonymous, Twelve-Step groups, and addiction treatment programs. All are examined from a biblical, historical, and research perspective. The book urges believers to trust the sufficiency of Christ and the Word of God instead of Twelve-Step and codependency/recovery theories and therapies.

If you would like a sample copy of a free newsletter regarding the intrusion of psychological counseling theories and therapies into the church, please write to:

PsychoHeresy Awareness Ministries
4137 Primavera Road
Santa Barbara, CA 93110